Leading: The Way

BEHAVIORS THAT DRIVE SUCCESS

Paulette Ashlin

OPEN BOOK
EDITIONS
A Berrett-Koehler Partner

LEADING: THE WAY
BEHAVIORS THAT DRIVE SUCCESS

iUniverse books may be ordered through booksellers or by contacting:

iUniverse
1663 Liberty Drive
Bloomington, IN 47403
www.iuniverse.com
1-800-Authors (1-800-288-4677)

Because of the dynamic nature of the Internet, any web addresses or links contained in this book may have changed since publication and may no longer be valid. The views expressed in this work are solely those of the author and do not necessarily reflect the views of the publisher, and the publisher hereby disclaims any responsibility for them.

Any people depicted in stock imagery provided by Thinkstock are models, and such images are being used for illustrative purposes only. Certain stock imagery © Thinkstock.

ISBN: 978-1-4917-9245-2 (sc)
ISBN: 978-1-4917-9246-9 (hc)
ISBN: 978-1-4917-9247-6 (e)

Library of Congress Control Number: 2016904792

Print information available on the last page.

iUniverse rev. date: 3/28/2016

Praise for
Leading: The Way—Behaviors That Drive Success

Research-based yet highly practical, *Leading: The Way* shows you how to transform your leadership style; communicate effectively up, down, and across; boost employee engagement; and exemplify vision and purpose. Get the complete picture of what's working, what's not working, and what you can do to improve from Paulette Ashlin's straightforward, behavior-based strategies! A terrific resource!

—Marshall Goldsmith, world-renowned executive coach and *New York Times* best-selling author of *Triggers*, *MOJO*, and *What Got You Here Won't Get You There*

Leading: The Way is a must-read for anyone aspiring to, or already in, a leadership position in the modern corporate world. *Leading: The Way*'s behavioral approach through self-assessment, empathy, vision, and followership in the context of global awareness has transformed my leadership abilities and will most certainly enhance yours.

—David A. Iannitti, MD, FACS, chief of Hepatic Pancreatic Biliary Surgery, program director of HPB Surgery Fellowship, and professor of surgery at Carolinas HealthCare System

Paulette Ashlin has leveraged her unique cultural upbringing and extensive business experience to write an outstanding book on leadership. She has woven decades of rigorous analysis with personal-best leadership stories to create a thorough yet easy-to-follow source for leadership development. *Leading: The Way* is a must-read whether you are an experienced executive looking to enhance your leadership skills or are a new manager embarking on your first significant leadership challenge.

—Geoffrey A. Peters, president and CEO of Wikoff Color Corporation

Leading: The Way reflects Paulette Ashlin's coaching style. It is a pragmatic, strategic, and realistic method to leadership success. The behavioral approach fills a gap in leadership development and builds upon competency and strengths models.

—Cathy Burns, president, Produce Marketing Association

Leadership retreats are a common practice for companies to invest in the growth of their leaders. Reading this book made me feel I went off-site to learn. The breadth of topics and depth of the insight was absorbing and transformative.

—Dr. Izzy Justice, chief talent officer, Premier Inc, author of *Epowerment* and *Triathlete EQ*

If you are a leader who wants to change, is able to change, and understands that changing behavior is a process, as stated by Paulette Ashlin, then her new book *Leading: The Way* is a must read. Paulette's fresh take on leading is inspirational and something to be enjoyed by all.

—Kristin Malbasa, vice president of human resources, MacLean-Fogg Component Solutions

This book is a deeply personal account of Paulette Ashlin's views on leadership, illustrated with relevant stories drawn from her successful coaching practice. Bottom line, it is a very accessible, behavioral approach to the challenging issues of effective leadership.

—John E. Kello, PhD, professor of psychology, Davidson College

Leading: The Way is the most clear, practical, and actionable business book I've ever read. Ms. Ashlin serves up the critical concepts of leadership in simple, bite-sized portions and brings each into razor-sharp focus using real-world examples—people and personalities we've all encountered in the workplace. Superb! Essential reading for anyone in business.

—Preston Fay, founder, Technekes

Paulette Ashlin has used her vast experience and knowledge to build a new road for leaders to travel if they are serious about making themselves and the organizations they serve achieve greater success. This book should be read by all who lead or aspire to.

—Harry L. Jones Sr., county manager (retired), Mecklenburg County (North Carolina)

In *Leading: The Way,* Paulette Ashlin effectively applies her experience from the board room to the manufacturing floor to give insight into the dynamics of how the real workplace functions. This guidance for improving business leaders is both inspired and practical coaching that's certain to improve skills in any business environment.

—John M. Schultz, general manager, Carmel Country Club

To my parents, the best coaches anyone could ever have. I am eternally grateful for your lifelong lessons, encouragement, wisdom, and love.

Contents

Introduction

Leaders aren't born, they are made.
And they are made just like anything else, through hard work.
—Vince Lombardi

I have always been an observer, even as a child. My family moved around a lot when I was growing up, literally skirting the globe and exposing me to a variety of different cultures that helped shape who I am today. At the age of eleven, I was propelled from a private French school to a US inner-city public school. Talk about culture shock! In my old world, uniforms and strict teachers were the norm, and the smartest kid in the class was also the most popular. I scarcely gave it a thought. But in my new world in America, everything was inside out and upside down. To be cool, kids showed off their clothes, not their intellect. Teachers were, by turns, friendly or disinterested or unpredictable. And the popular kids? Suffice to say that popularity in my new school had nothing to do with academic ability or classroom achievements.

I scrambled to conform to my new city, culture, customs, and classes. I'd like to say that, being a resilient kid, I adapted quickly, but I did not. Oh, I wanted to have friends. I wanted to be liked. I wanted to be respected and acknowledged. I wanted to be held in high regard and to have influence. But my initial attempts at befriending others failed. I spoke English fluently because my dad was American, but I didn't understand what my American classmates were saying even though we spoke the same language. Slang words, different idioms, and a completely alien take on things struck me as strange. The more

I observed and tried to fit in, the stranger things became. I got good at observing nonverbal cues—body language, if you will—and I was able to figure out a path I could follow. I gradually became fascinated with behavior, and that fascination still holds today.

The one thing going in my favor was that I was a child who liked to get to the bottom of life's dilemmas. Introspective and results oriented, I made a practice of regarding my surroundings more keenly. I dug in. I wasn't included? Oh well. Not being included gave me perspective. And as I watched people more carefully, I realized that my classmates tended to cluster in groups based on similarities in demographics, looks, socioeconomic class, and intellect. Moreover, the individuals in those groups tended to mirror one another. They behaved similarly— sometimes, identically. Their behavior defined them. Their *behavior* was the key to how they were regarded and what they were able to accomplish.

I now know that this phenomenon isn't restricted to teenagers. But at the time, recognizing the influence of behavior was a revelation to me. The way certain people stuck to one another was intriguing to me, albeit also disconcerting because it became difficult to penetrate certain cliques. The concept of cliques is also known as *tribalism* and is present in some corporate cultures. It can be deadly in terms of cooperation, productivity, and profitability within the company. A good leader will recognize tribalism and do everything possible to defeat this very real and natural human tendency. Once I identified behaviors of the people around me, it made it easier to determine whom I wanted to be, wanted to be with, and wanted to be like. It made it easier for me to make my way.

In a simplistic way, fitting in was my first scientific, albeit primitive, research. I took note of the people I admired and wanted to emulate. I also observed people I disliked and would never want to imitate. And I didn't limit my observational study group to classmates. I expanded my observations to include teachers, businesspeople, celebrities, clergy, and, of course and most importantly, my parents. I watched people's actions, behaviors, and facial expressions and tried to reconcile what they *said* with what they *did*.

Many years later, the observational skills I sharpened for survival as an adolescent served me well as an executive in the boardrooms of corporate America, where much of what I observed didn't make sense. I saw corporate executives who were smart and kind but not held in high regard. I saw leaders who achieved a certain level of success but were held in disdain by their teams and colleagues. I saw people who were well educated and well traveled but who couldn't inspire. And likewise, I saw people with the weakest of résumés and credentials who seemed to inspire legions to produce and excel.

What is the secret of professional success? For anybody? What is that magic formula that will propel you to ultimate professional and personal success? How do people become and, more importantly, *remain* leaders? From my over a decade of executive coaching, I have concluded that behavior is indeed a defining element of success and failure in a leadership role. This book is aimed at managers as well as high-level executives. But if you are new in your career or are an entry-level individual, this book serves as a guide to your future as you become a leader yourself. The book is organized around core concepts of self-awareness, self-control, humility, integrity, empathy, global intelligence, personal stewardship, and performance. I will use personal anecdotes to illustrate some of these core concepts that are central to my behavior-based philosophy of leadership success.

One of the most defining moments for me as an executive coach was when I realized that great leaders are also great actors. They are great performers. They know how to act, how to perform, and, in a nutshell, how to behave—how to behave appropriately.

A client of mine recently asked me to consider why I am writing this book. It is, after all, a considerable undertaking, requiring time from my work and my friends and family. But I've always known that this is a book that I'd need to write, because as simple as it sounds, *I want people to be happy at work.*

I studied psychology and received my masters in industrial/organizational psychology. As an executive coach, I work with companies and leaders around the world, to help those leaders become more successful and effective. I am not so naive as to believe that "bliss" ensures corporate success, of course. But I do know that when a leader is successful and effective, his or her workplace and team become more productive, more disciplined, more focused, and, yes, more content—happy—in their work environment. Moreover, I know that many corporate efforts and coaching trends—with the same goals of creating a more productive, more disciplined, and more focused workplace—fall short for a number of reasons.

Where most leadership literature focuses on leadership competencies (like character and integrity), my intention is to go a step beyond and describe the *behaviors* that support and sustain those competencies. What you'll find here are general principles of effective leadership drawn from my colleagues' and my consulting experience, supported by research. Indeed, you'll find a comprehensive bibliography in the back of the book that may be of interest should you desire to do your own research. The anecdotes I use in the book are based on real experiences. Of course, I changed the names to protect the privacy of the individuals involved. The important point is that the stories will help you more easily understand the situations that come up where behavior really counts, both on a negative and on a positive level.

While not an academic text, this book is for leaders who understand and are willing to change their behaviors to become the best they can be. By and large, most of my clients are high achieving and well intentioned. Even more than their bosses or boards of directors, they themselves want to be better, more effective leaders. And on their journeys to do so, most, somewhere in their careers, have undergone various "assessments."

Because you are reading this book, I'm betting that you too have undergone assessments, either to identify your strengths and skill sets or perhaps to assess your personality or to delineate your competencies. If so, you likely were intrigued by the results. The difference, however, between identifying those behaviors and then *changing* those behaviors is vast.

You likely have already realized that it's not enough to *know* your strengths and weaknesses. Instead, you need to understand how to *behave* your way into more-effective behaviors. Sounds pretty simple, right? If you act like a great leader, your actual behavior will begin to change for the better as the acting becomes second nature.

Assessments are important, of course, but they are only a first step. Some assessments, for example, measure competencies like inquisitiveness or prudence, which is good to know. But test results aren't solutions. They are information. And while self-knowledge is informative, this book is not only about informing. It's about responding, changing, and improving. It's about behavior. It's about pulling out strengths that need to be exhibited and about squelching the tendencies that impede effective leadership.

From my years of observation and coaching, I know that the one factor that most differentiates effective leaders from ineffective leaders is *behavior*. Not education. Not experience. Not motivation. Not family history. And certainly not good intentions. (As one of my colleagues often says, "The road to hell is paved with good intentions.")

And here's the good news: behavior, unlike some of those other factors, is something you can control and change. You just have to be willing to make the change.

Great leaders behave in great ways. The key to being a great leader isn't luck or being gifted or highly educated or unusually driven. The key to being a great leader is behavior. *Great leaders behave in great ways.*

Sometimes, taking the first step in a journey is the hardest. You have to psych yourself up to get started, but once you do, there is joy and enlightenment in the journey itself. The outcome, what you get when you reach your destination, is hopefully something you've worked hard for. Let's take that first step together! You're already on your way to becoming an even better leader than you are now.

Chapter 1

Follow the Leader

People buy into the leader before they buy into the vision.
—John Maxwell

Behave well, and people will follow you to the ends of the earth. Behave poorly, and ... well, the headlines are littered with examples of leaders who lost everything in the wake of bad behavior. The Enron disaster is one of many examples of how things can go wrong in a hurry if the people at the top of a company misbehave. The scale of the misbehavior doesn't have to be as grand as was the case with Enron either. Companies can die the death of a thousand cuts, those little transgressions in leadership that ultimately undermine the entire organization. I coach my clients to understand that behavior is something they can control. You can't control genetics, you can't control IQ, you can't control situations or the economy or world events or stock prices, but *you can control your behavior.* You can choose to be a good leader, and you can choose to be an even better leader. It's that simple.

If you are already a successful leader, you'll surely recognize many of the situations I describe in these pages, and you should find affirmation of behaviors that have led to your success. If you're an aspiring leader, you'll find specific lessons and tips for altering your behavior to help you get to the next level—whatever that may be.

1

Whether you are leading a team of three or a company of thousands, leadership is a huge privilege. Although only a rarefied few realize it, you, as a leader, have incredible power to make or break a person's day, to elevate or destroy someone with a few words or behaviors. And in my eyes, that power comes with responsibility: a leader is obligated to lead by constructive and noble behavior.

For some people, leadership comes naturally. These rare individuals already know how to attract followers (an essential component of leadership) and inspire those followers to ever-increasing levels of productivity and innovation.

Most of the time, though, leadership doesn't come naturally. Good intentions and cognitive thoughts don't automatically translate into the actions of successful leadership. And the actions that got you to where you are will not always work as you scale the executive ladder. For example, as an individual contributor, you might execute assignments yourself. When you become a leader of many people and departments, you simply do not have the capacity to personally take on all those individual assignments. You execute and implement through others. And your behavior either motivates them or turns them off.

Followership

The crux of the matter is that great leaders are wonderful at inspiring others to follow. It's not like you're the Pied Piper luring innocent children on a perilous journey that doesn't end well. You are a person people look up to. They choose to follow you because you instill confidence. You show others through your behavior that you are self-aware, that you possess self-control, that you're humble when necessary, and that you are empathetic even when the chips are down and your stress levels are blowing through the roof. You inspire because you communicate effectively, imparting your big-picture vision of the company's way forward in a clear and concise manner.

You'll sometimes hear the concept referred to as *followership*. The concept can make some people uncomfortable, but I am by no means comparing human beings to sheep! The concept is larger than that, in that the very definition of *leading* requires that someone be *following*. In this sense, increasing your followership is a very positive and natural thing. A successful leader understands that followership isn't a given. It doesn't automatically accompany a title or position. Followership comes when it has been earned. Great leaders behave with *integrity* and *empathy* and *humility*. They have *self-awareness* and *self-control*. They embrace the notions of *self-stewardship* and *global intelligence* and *acting* like a successful leader. They are great *communicators*. They understand the power, influence, and effects of their own behavior. Likewise, they understand that, without these behaviors, effective leadership is impossible.

Let's take a closer look at the ramifications of certain behavioral shortfalls when you are a leader working hard to create a more profitable company.

> A lack of *self-awareness* leads to embarrassment, inappropriate behavior, and misalignment between self and business.

> A lack of *self-control* leads to childish behavior and impulsive conduct and thus regret and energy wasted on damage control.

> A lack of *empathy* leads to narcissism and detrimental all-about-me behavior.

> A lack of *humility* leads to tunnel vision in an attempt to win and a loss of others' wisdom.

> A lack of *integrity* leads to wariness, skepticism, and lawsuits.

A lack of *personal stewardship* leads to personal and professional implosion and meltdown.

A lack of *communication* leads to confusion and chaos.

A lack of *global intelligence* leads to stagnation.

A lack of *performing* leads to the inability to move forward.

Aristotle said, "We are what we repeatedly do. Excellence, then, is not an act, but a habit." I say, "The more you behave in a certain way, the more you become it."

Behavioral conditioning

Behaviorism, also known as behavioral psychology, is based on the idea that all behaviors are acquired through conditioning. Conditioning occurs through interaction with the environment and is affected by positive and negative reinforcement. Behaviorists believe that our responses to environmental stimuli shape our behaviors. In other words, we behave in a certain way because we are rewarded for that behavior.

For example, if I change my behavior and stop eating my favorite dessert—chocolate mousse with whipped cream—I will be rewarded with weight loss. The reward of losing weight perpetuates the behavior of avoiding sweets.

We will also behave in certain ways to avoid punishment. For example, leaders who will not relinquish control through delegation or empowerment perpetuate a culture of low risk. I have worked with leaders who complain that their teams do not take initiative, only to discover that it is because these same leaders tear their people apart if something is not done in exactly the way the way they wanted.

Renowned American psychologist and behaviorist B. F. Skinner believed that all human action was the direct result of conditioning. You likely are familiar with his famous research where he influenced and predicted the behavior of rats based on whether the animals received positive or negative reinforcement. Over a series of many studies, Skinner found that the rats would alter their behavior, intentionally moving a small lever, either to get a reward (food) or to avoid discomfort (a slight electrical current). Now, I don't mean to compare any of you to rats, but the point is this: when we *behave* in a certain way, we can, predictably, earn positive results. In a corporate setting, these results might be a financial gain, a return on investment, increased productivity, or a more efficient and happy workplace.

And remember that the beauty of this approach to executive coaching is that, unlike your genetics, background, education, or other predispositions, behavior is something you can change, provided

- you are motivated enough to change;
- you realize positive rewards for the changes; and
- you know how to change.

This book can help you change.

In the movie *Batman Begins*, Rachel says to Bruce Wayne (Batman), "It's not what you are underneath, it's what you *do* that defines you." My point exactly! Successful leaders walk the talk. Their actions and attitudes inspire and motivate others. And in an unexpected twist, it doesn't really matter what they are thinking, how they are feeling, or what their intentions are. It is their actions—their *behaviors*—that influence others.

If you are in a hurry and move quickly to your destination without making eye contact with those around you, people might think you are snobbish and arrogant. You might be neither—just late, distracted, and anxious about your meeting. Or you might be in pain or upset about a personal matter. But if you smile and genuinely engage others, they will react to your good demeanor and find you appealing.

A relatively new president of a $4-billion organization confided in me that his right-hand person, someone on whom he relied for executing the company's challenging mission, was starting to derail. Disheartened, the president told me, "I've received feedback that Bob is leading through intimidation, trying to scare people, using his high position, and acting like a big bully. Bob's been a valuable teammate—a mover and a shaker—but I can't tolerate a bully on my staff. Can you help Bob? *Can you get him to change?*"

Yes. I firmly believe that most leaders are perfectly capable of changing their behaviors and sustaining the new behaviors. The choice is theirs. If a leader is not willing to change his or her behavior, if that leader is not intrinsically or extrinsically motivated to do so, he or she will not. It is as simple as that.

However, a leader must be open to change and, I hope it goes without saying, able to change his or her behavior. The behaviorist approach for business coaching is not suitable for individuals with behavioral or personality disorders. An unwillingness to change behaviors is just as big a hurdle. As acclaimed football coach Vince Lombardi famously noted, "Leaders aren't born, they are made. And they are made just like anything else, through hard work."

Marshall Goldsmith, in his book *Triggers*, says, "No one can make us change unless we want to change." He further concludes, "When we dive all the way into adult behavioral change—with 100% focus and energy—we become an irresistible force rather than the proverbial immovable project."

Of course, the way you think and the way you feel may have some influence over your success in leadership, but it is what you do—your behavior—that is experienced by those around you. Although it does help me to understand a client's motivation and what is going on in his or her head, I find that by the time I come into the picture, clients are at a point in their lives and careers where it is more productive to reshape any unwanted behavior and to enhance the successful behaviors.

It is your behavior that impacts the people around you in the workplace and in your personal lives. You may be well intentioned, highly educated, and extremely intelligent. But it is only your behavior that is observed by others, so it is your behavior that must be changed, adapted, modified, or refined to propel you to success.

In his wildly successful book *What Got You Here Won't Get You There,* Marshall Goldsmith says that one of the troubles with success is that our previous success often prevents us from achieving more success. Think about that: our *previous success* prevents us from achieving *more success.* That's because people continue to behave in a manner that yields the reinforcement they've typically received over the years. Sometimes, they don't realize that behavior requirements have changed for their current environment and certainly for their next steps. In Bob's case, it was apparent to me that, somehow, Bob had been rewarded for his behavior over the years. After all, he was the second-in-command of a large organization, and he must have done something right to ascend to this level.

The 360-degree feedback process

To better understand any coaching situation, I first gather information (actual and perceived) about the leader. I call this the 360-degree feedback process, where I look full circle around a leader and interview the individuals around him or her—whether they be managers or colleagues or subordinates. This background allows me to be in the game—pardon the cliché—helping me see how others perceive the individual, how he or she leads, and what workplace dynamics are in play. I typically interview ten to twenty people around my coaching clients. During the structured interviews, I ask questions and probe about all aspects of leadership. I compile the information into a composite report that I then offer to my coaching client.

If conducted tactfully, honestly, and with high emotional intelligence, the 360-degree feedback process is like holding up a mirror to someone. After collecting data, I meet with my coaching client and reveal the raw data—the good and the bad. It is truly like when you hold up a mirror to glance at the back of your head; you see what you thought you knew so well—all the blind spots.

As I conducted 360-degree interviews with Bob, the president, and other key people, I recognized a pattern: the behavior that was holding Bob back was the same behavior that had contributed to his success. By being aggressive, dominant, outspoken, and narrow-minded, he'd been regarded as a go-getter, hustling up the corporate ladder, earning one promotion after the other. The company had rewarded him for his exemplary financial results and execution by promoting him every few years, so he'd received the message that it was perfectly okay to behave as he had, managing and leading people through fear, threats, and intimidation.

He even demeaned subordinates in meetings, snickering and making snide comments. Since no one ever addressed the inappropriateness of such behavior, Bob subconsciously believed that this was the way leaders behaved in order to succeed. From his perspective, he was doing everything just right. From a behaviorist's vantage point, Bob's situation was pretty much Psych 101. Bob's negative behavior was positively rewarded, albeit unwittingly, every time he was promoted. His behavior was not, however, the type of behavior that could successfully sustain a leader. To continue on his leadership path—and indeed, to stay with the company—Bob had to begin changing his behavior. Immediately.

Not everyone has the opportunity or luxury of having a coach come in to interview his or her inner and outer circles. You can still, however, change your behavior on your own by following the recommendations in this book, by looking long and hard at the way you currently behave and seeking the impressions and opinions of those around you. You can follow the same steps I do as I coach corporate executives. You can assess your current behavior. You can ask others about the job you're doing. You can establish your own advisory board—of colleagues, family, clients, employers—to give you honest, fair feedback. We'll talk more about the feedback loop a bit later.

Fishbowl leadership

> Become the kind of leader that people would follow voluntarily,
> even if you had no title or position.
> —Brian Tracy

I often explain to my coaching clients that when they are in leadership roles, they are basically in a fishbowl. People are watching them, so their actions, behaviors, and communications need to be exceptionally transparent and clear. Frequent communication of the same message can help validate and back up others' perception of a leader's integrity. Again, for most leaders, the problem isn't an actual lack of integrity. It's a matter of perception, which means that behaving with integrity requires a certain degree of self-awareness, self-control, humility, and empathy.

Let me give you a simple and real example that a client brought to my attention. Two colleagues—male and female—travel to a client meeting in Manhattan. Naturally, they travel together, attend the meeting together, and take their meals together. But they're in the Big Apple—should they go to a dance club together after work? This is where it gets a bit sticky—not because there is anything wrong per se in going to a dance club together but because doing so could be perceived as inappropriate behavior, especially if both individuals are not at the same level within the company. The two colleagues have to have the self-awareness to realize how their actions can appear and to act to avoid the perception of lack of integrity.

At other times, leaders—highly ethical leaders—are not highly regarded (and remember, being highly regarded translates into being highly followed) because they are, to put it simply, too quiet. Because these leaders are rather low-key, their followers don't know them well. When leaders aren't understood, their integrity comes into question. Which is to say that it isn't enough to have integrity; I urge my clients to show their integrity, to put it on display. To behave overtly with integrity.

Take another common example. Let's say a company is about to make a significant, life-altering change. Perhaps the company is about to restructure. Perhaps the company is moving to new offices. Perhaps it is about to make a stock offering. For various reasons, the leadership cannot, for legal reasons, discuss their intentions with their employees. But the leadership is in a fishbowl. The management team can't swim in the shadows. It's impossible. So what happens next?

Leadership tries to keep the news quiet, *but*, inevitably and invariably, word—at least part of it—gets out. Employees get a whiff that change is underfoot. They don't have full details. Whispers turn into rumors that swirl into accusations that blossom into quiet but widespread panic. Even when well-meaning leaders finally reveal the "happy" announcement, the news is undermined by earlier worries and innuendoes. And the damage is done. Despite the eventual announcement of "good" news, leadership is regarded as sneaky, secretive, untrustworthy, and, sadly, lacking integrity. Since leaders are in a fishbowl and are observed even more intensely during times of uncertainty, they can—and should— behave in a reassuring manner. Communication needs to intensify during these times when, ironically, leaders feel they have less time to communicate. Being bound by legal documents and confidentiality does not preclude leaders from admitting to the organization that changes are upcoming. In fact, principles of change management dictate that the organization and its leaders implement a thoughtful communications plan.

In conclusion, the behavior-based approach to improving leadership effectiveness is both unique and highly doable. Of all the things you can control, your behavior is one of the most easily changed aspects of your personal and work life. Your followers will notice if you misbehave, and they will notice if you behave well. They will also notice changes for the better or for the worse. Remember, the big fish in the fishbowl can never swim in the shadows. The light of day will always be present, as it should be.

Leadership roundup

A behavior-based approach to leadership does not focus on education, personal drive, or intelligence. Instead, the focus is on how you act. What you say and how you say it influences the nature of your corporate culture. A positive corporate culture leads to interdepartmental cooperation, reduces duplicated efforts that lead to wasted resources, boosts productivity, encourages innovation, heightens employee morale, and often bolsters profitability. All of these are worthy goals that can be achieved through a behavior-based leadership style.

- Leaders need followers. Without them, you can't lead. Your behavior impacts either positively or negatively the people who follow you.
- Behavior often results from conditioning. Positive or negative feedback can create a pattern of behavior. Recognizing the positive and negative inputs will enable you to change your behavior.
- Feedback is essential in identifying what behaviors are negatively impacting the followers in your company. The 360-degree feedback process can identify these behaviors.
- As a leader, you're operating in a fishbowl. All eyes are upon you. Therefore, your behavior, even down to how you dress and what time you come to work in the morning, are all up for scrutiny among your followers. If you change your behavior for the better, your followers will notice.

Chapter 2

Self-Awareness

He who knows others is wise.
He who knows himself is enlightened.
—Laozi

I once had the pleasure of working with a remarkable leader, Mike. A former marine, Mike was well organized, results oriented, approachable, and not surprisingly, given his military training, his posture was perfect and precise. There was, however, an obvious disconnect between Mike and his superiors. His team, who knew him well and worked with him on a daily basis, enjoyed and appreciated his management style. His superiors, however, including board members and longtime clients, weren't comfortable with Mike. And while Mike recognized that there was some kind of problem, he couldn't put his finger on it.

The best leaders are self-aware. They know how their behaviors affect others, where their voices echo, and how their words are interpreted. They control their moods. They know who they are. Just as important, they know how they are perceived. If you cultivate your own sense of self-awareness, you'll see that awareness translate into behavior patterns that reinforce positive feedback in your organization from the top down. The positive reinforcement will lead to increased productivity among your followers, higher morale, less turnover, better client relations, and a happier work environment for everyone. Companies with positive corporate cultures tend to be more profitable than those that foster negativity by virtue of the climate leaders promote. Mike was introspective—he had a profound understanding of his strengths and weaknesses. What he didn't understand was how his behavior was perceived by others.

In a way, it doesn't make sense. If you see yourself, then you know how others see you, right? The problem is that our perceptions of ourselves can be distorted. For example, whereas I might perceive myself as assertive and confident, my actual behavior might lead others to perceive me as controlling and abrasive. Or, on the other hand, I may believe I am reserved, quiet, and wise. But my colleagues might perceive me as dispassionate, aloof, or even arrogant. And if we don't see ourselves accurately—if we're not open to seeing ourselves accurately—how can we hope to understand how others see us?

Self-awareness is not merely understanding our strengths and weaknesses. Nor is it simply the ability to identify, recognize, and understand our emotions, motivators, and behaviors. Self-awareness is bigger than that. It is understanding the impact we have on the people around us. It is the first step in exuding influence.

There are two components to self-awareness. First is knowing yourself and having a deep understanding of your strengths, weaknesses, limitations, emotional makeup, and triggers. Not surprisingly, many leaders have this type of self-awareness in spades. They've paid just enough attention and have worked on themselves just enough to know themselves—if only on a superficial level. There may be a few blind spots, but in general, these leaders can describe themselves fairly accurately. But that's only half of the formula, and for a business leader, it's the least important half.

The second, more profound component of self-awareness is understanding how you are perceived. This is where most leaders fail. Indeed, it's where most of us fall short. We may know ourselves really well but have misconceptions about how other people know us.

Of the leadership behaviors I identify in this book, none is more essential than the accumulation of self-awareness. Without self-awareness, how can one have self-control? Without self-awareness, how can one be empathetic or humble? Without self-awareness, how can one hope to master *any* behavior that will lead to greater effectiveness in the workplace? The simple answer is you can't. Self-awareness is integral to your success as a leader.

The best leaders seem to be naturally introspective. They know themselves really well, *and* they know how they are regarded. With this knowledge, they understand how to modulate their behavior for maximum effect. In other words, by knowing themselves, they are able to create desirable outcomes from others.

Think of it this way. Do you look at yourself in the mirror every morning? Of course you do. I honestly don't know anyone who doesn't. We are social animals, in environments in which we are surrounded by other people. It's only natural that we want to know how others see us. Most of us care what others think of us—up to a point, of course. We know that how we look and behave affects how people treat us and respond to us and to our behavior. We want to know how we appear. And since our appearance affects our environment, altering our appearance can also alter our environment—to our benefit or to our detriment.

As acclaimed author and psychologist Daniel Goleman noted, "If your emotional abilities aren't in hand, if you don't have self-awareness, if you are not able to manage your distressing emotions, if you can't have empathy and have effective relationships, then no matter how smart you are, you are not going to get very far."

It all begins, of course, with self-awareness—the single most fundamental attribute of a successful leader.

Liabilities of low self-awareness

> The most difficult thing in life is to know yourself.
> —Thales

So when you looked in the mirror this morning, what did you see? Was the reflection accurate? Is it possible you overlooked something? Think about it. You *see* yourself so often that the image might be distorted. Could you have somehow missed a few stray hairs or perhaps uneven sideburns? Or maybe you didn't miss anything at all and instead saw flaws that aren't actually there?

You can see how easily that could happen. Think, for example, of beautiful teenage girls who look in a mirror and see only magnified flaws. A pretty teen girl who sees imperfection where none exists might think she's overweight. This negative self-perception can lead to eating disorders, which can sometimes be fatal. At the very least, the distorted self-view can create deep-seated psychological problems that will impact every aspect of her life. The same thing can happen in the corporate world. An overinflated sense of self can lead to pomposity, arrogance, insensitivity, and a distinct inability to work in a team setting. A self-loathing or even a low sense of self-confidence can lead to ineffectual performance and can turn into a self-fulfilling prophecy of failure, because others will sense the inferiority complex. People are like dogs and fear. Our bosses and colleagues can smell fear of failure a mile away, and they don't want to be associated with individuals who exude such vibes. Thus, a lack of self-esteem and a fixation on one's imperfections can translate into actual failure because others can sense that in us on an almost visceral level.

Our perceptions of ourselves can be distorted—by our background, our experiences, or even our actual eyesight. And if we do not see ourselves clearly, how do we know what other people see?

We all have blind spots, particularly when it comes to ourselves. When my daughters were young, I reveled in fixing their hair. For me, it was never a chore. Whether simply combing and brushing or braiding and tucking those soft wavy locks into buns and ponytails, I enjoyed it all. Like all children, however, as my girls grew older, they resisted my efforts. They wanted to do it themselves. By the time they were teenagers, they were pretty vocal about me leaving their hair alone. In a feeble effort to change their minds, I pointed out, "But you can't see the back of your head! Let me fix it."

Those of you with teenagers won't be surprised to learn that my plea fell on deaf ears. My point, however, was valid. My daughters couldn't see the backs of their heads. Yes, it was their hair and their heads, but they couldn't see what I could see. They couldn't see what others could see—the very definition of *blind spot*.

It's the same in the workplace. We have blind spots. We behave a certain way and think that we know how we're coming across, but that's not always the case. We don't see ourselves clearly, so we don't always project the way we want to be perceived.

I have worked with leaders who are astoundingly strategic but whose behaviors and communication projected only tactical knowledge. Some of my clients are supremely self-confident, but their behaviors gave the impression that they were hesitant or not trustworthy. These perceptions were a shock to my clients, who did not quite realize how they were coming across. Like most people, they couldn't see their blind spots.

Janet, a no-nonsense executive, shattered glass ceiling after glass ceiling at a large retail company. It was tough going, but by being fierce and focused, she was rewarded with promotions and bonuses and ultimately was named company president. She basked in being known as "one tough cookie," feeling that this style of leadership was admired and respected. Janet's perception of herself was crystal clear. She saw herself as focused and driven but fair and respected.

In time, a new CEO arrived on the scene—a man known for being accommodating and gracious. He expected Janet to adapt to his others-first leadership style, but Janet clung to what had made her successful. She couldn't see any downside to her tough-cookie reputation. That was when I was called in to conduct a series of 360-degree interviews. When I compiled the results and held the metaphorical mirror up to Janet, she cringed. Her idea of "tough cookie" didn't fit with the way her peers and teammates regarded her. Where Janet thought she was seen as focused and driven, her associates saw her as cutthroat and uncaring—highly undesirable traits in a leader.

Janet lacked self-awareness. She didn't understand herself, and she had no sense of how she was regarded by the people around her. These two things were leading to her certain downfall.

During the series of 360-degree interviews I conducted with eighteen of Janet's colleagues, I asked one of my routine questions: "If it weren't for her title, would you follow Janet over a hill, not knowing what's on the other side?"

What I'm hoping to hear when I ask this question is a resounding "Yes!" But in this instance, a shocking sixteen of the eighteen interviewees replied, "No." When I shared the news, Janet was devastated. She knew her strengths and weakness. She knew how she behaved. But she didn't realize how out of sync her behaviors were with the evolving organization. She had no idea that her followers had so little confidence in her. Talk about blind spots!

Identifying your blind spots

> The need to prove who you are
> will vanish once you know who you are.
> —Danielle Pierre

It takes self-awareness to identify your blind spots. It also requires a willingness to probe for answers when you may think none are needed. How you go about this depends on your personal preferences, but in all approaches introspection is the key. After that, communication comes into play. Recall that I mentioned having your own advisory board can help you become a better leader. The advisory board concept entails asking colleagues, friends, and family for feedback. Pay attention to the answers you receive. You don't necessarily need an executive coach like me, though coaches can be very helpful. What you do need is a commitment to enhance your self-awareness and a willingness to change your behavior if any negativity is detected.

Let's take a look at introspection in a bit more detail. After all, it is the first step to becoming self-aware. You can't process positive and negative feedback from others if you aren't able to take a good hard look at yourself in the privacy of your own thoughts.

My friend's daughter was a rather quiet, introspective little ballerina. You may be envious, thinking that a reserved child is easier to parent, but my friend was always keenly aware that her child could come across as snobbish or arrogant because she was so quiet. My friend often reminded her daughter throughout high school that she may not be perceived the way she intended. Quiet people often are unaware of how others interpret their silence. Knowing that silence can be mistaken for inattention or disinterest, though, my friend's daughter had to make a deliberate effort to speak up and participate in social settings. Once she got to college, she no longer had to make the effort. Being outgoing and talkative became second nature. She changed her behavior.

I recently conducted a 360-degree interview on behalf of one of the most self-aware people I know. Adam knows himself well, is very comfortable in his own skin, and is accepting of the fact that he is, by nature, extremely quiet and reserved. What Adam doesn't know is that his tendency to be a man of few words has been misinterpreted as being a man of few cares— the exact opposite of how Adam wants to be perceived.

The 360-degree interviews conducted by executive coaches (like me) are one of many ways to evaluate a leader's degree of self-awareness. Basic assessment tools—including variations of emotional quotient (EQ) tests, the Predictive Index (PI), Hogan assessments, and the Meyers–Briggs Type Indicator (MBTI)—can also be found online. Any of us can take one in the privacy of our home or office and compare the results with what we *thought* we were like.

To be a good coach, I have to be in the game. An assessment allows a coach to get up to speed quickly and understand a client's strengths and behaviors. The DISC model of behavior, initially developed by William Mouton Marston, a physiological psychologist with a PhD from Harvard, is a standby in my profession. Marston identified four neutral—not good or bad—behavioral emotions. These four types— dominance (D), inducement (I, now often referred to as influence), submission (S, often referred to as steadiness), and compliance (C)—are parts of all of our behaviors. The key is to determine which of these behaviors capture an individual's "style." The DISC results tell us more about our own styles, and the more we understand about ourselves, the better we can identify our strengths and work on areas of weakness.

As a behaviorist, I find some of these assessments to be very matter of fact. I regard them similarly to basic medical checkups—an opportunity to take a person's behavioral temperature, so to speak, on a regular basis. As with a medical checkup, you have to be open and honest. You have to be willing to understand that each of us has areas needing improvement and areas of strength. You have to be willing to look more deeply at yourself and see yourself as others see you.

Not every leader, however, has the confidence to look in the metaphorical mirror. I'm working now with a CEO, Ray, who sees great value in increasing self-awareness across his team. Indeed, he is quite the fan. Ray wants everyone on his team to participate in a standard behavior assessment. He's pushing his team members to understand their own individual leadership styles, so they can behave more effectively as individuals, as a team, and as human beings. Since Ray is such a huge proponent of behavioral assessments, I worked quickly to begin scheduling. The assessment I recommended for his team—the DISC—can be quickly administered. With it, there are no right or wrong answers. There are no good or bad results. The DISC simply provides insights about an individual in four neutral categories: dominance, influence, steadiness, and compliance. These insights help individuals see where they can work (lead and manage) more effectively.

Pretty easy, right? Sure it is. Except for Ray. As it turned out, I couldn't get the assessment on Ray's schedule. It became apparent that he was dodging the issue, even joking about it. Ray is fairly self-aware, and as a result, he realized that while he wanted his employees to see themselves more clearly, he himself was afraid to do the same.

After all the teasing, I finally confronted Ray. His behavior was clearly inconsistent, but he would not budge. "I don't want to know, Paulette. I'm pretty darned confident that whatever I've been doing is what has made me successful. So yes, I'll take the assessment. But I don't want to see the results. *Because the truth is, I don't want to change.*"

Learning the truth about oneself can be scary, but it's the very first step in becoming a more effective leader. I can't help Ray understand and work with others until he is willing to understand himself, so I'm encouraging him to regard the assessment as routine self-maintenance. Like so many leaders, Ray has blind spots. It's not enough for his team to confide in me. He has to be willing to hear the information for himself.

"What you're doing now is like shaving without a mirror," I've said. "You've been doing it a long time, so you're pretty sure you're doing a fine job. But the only way to be certain is to check in the mirror to see if you've missed any spots. You need that reflection—feedback—to close the gap between what you *think* you accomplished and what you *actually* accomplished."

Only after taking a long, hard, honest look at yourself can you begin to understand yourself and, even more important in the workplace, understand how you are perceived by others. The very process of working to identify your blind spots will boost your self-awareness. That, in turn, will (hopefully) exert a positive influence on how you behave as a leader, thereby boosting employee productivity and morale. In short, you'll be taking the right steps to get the most out of your followers.

Enhancing your self-awareness

> The first thing you have to know is yourself.
> A man who knows himself can step outside himself and
> watch his own reactions like an observer.
> —Adam Smith

I have found, personally, that the mere anticipation of undergoing a 360-degree process or soliciting feedback from my clients propels me to change or enhance some of my behaviors. I make myself behave in ways that might generate positive feedback. This is all very natural. It is almost like touching up your hair as a reflex *before* you actually look in the mirror. How many times have we all done that?

When I hold up that mirror to others—the consolidated results of interviews or assessments—reactions range from "That sounds familiar" to "I had no idea!" Then, predictably, comes the concern. As one client poignantly said, "I wish someone had told me all this ten or fifteen years ago."

Ultimately, though, nearly everyone asks, "How can I fix this?"

That willingness to address the issue head-on is the behavior of a leader with great potential. The interviews and assessments are merely diagnostic. Without a willingness to take action, the data is useless. Still, it can be overwhelming, so I encourage clients to be happy with their areas of strength and to zero in on areas for improvement, allowing a few months for real, measurable change. Increasing self-awareness takes time, and as I tell my clients, there is an actual *art* to it, which works perfectly into a memorable acronym for increasing self-awareness:

ART
- Ask.
- Reach.
- Take action.

Ask. Even without a coach, you can gather feedback. As I've said, making a habit of asking trusted coworkers, current and former bosses, and team members about your professional brand and behavior is almost certainly going to help you get a better sense of how others perceive you. With that information in hand, you can become more self-aware. Be open and willing to listen, and ask people to be entirely honest. Ask general questions like "Do people think I understand them?" and "When I make presentations, am I viewed as credible?" You can also ask specific questions, such as "How did that meeting go?" "How was my body language?" and "Could you tell when I got irritated or disinterested or confused?" One client asked, "Does my voice resonate when I speak up in a meeting, or does it quiver?"

What you're doing is getting a "reflection" of yourself. You're trying to understand how other people see you, and to get an accurate representation, it is important that you get the perspective of more than one person.

That's why I encourage my clients to create their own advisory board of trusted associates with varying personalities, education, and professions. As you might expect, asking too many questions too often can make a leader come across as insecure, so it may help to give your questions some context. Before asking a question, you might say, "I just read a book about self-awareness, and it got me thinking about how people might view me." Or, "I've been told that I can come across as talkative [or quiet or overbearing or so on], and I'm curious how that comes across in meetings like these."

Reach. It is not enough to ask a few trusted work colleagues to share their insights. Increasing self-awareness requires multiple perspectives—reaching outside of the workplace for the perspective of friends, spouses, and family members. Having a board of advisers that extends outside the walls of your business allows you to get the opinions of the people who know you best and are willing to provide the honest type of feedback that others might not. Naturally, you will want to tap into their subject matter expertise. So if you have a friend whose specialty is finance, you may run your P&L statement by him or her. The same goes for people who excel in interpersonal relationships. You might bounce off an idea that has to do with corporate politics.

Take action. Stop and consider how your behavior might impact not only the people around you but also your business and bottom line. Much of this step involves empathy, which I'll cover later in this book, but being self-aware often requires taking your time and paying attention to your behavior. After all, if you don't pause and notice your behavior, how can you hope to change it? Create an action plan to address the behaviors you want to modify, enhance, or even eliminate. My clients construct a coaching action plan comprised of strengths, two to four behaviors they want to enhance or modify, and a description of the ways they are going to measure the changes in behavior. The very act of writing makes an impression on our brains that will help reinforce our underlying motives, and it will also make it more likely that we'll follow our action plans.

Advocates of actually writing your goals and plans down frequently cite a well-known written-goal study from Harvard. For example, Mark McCormack mentions it in his book *What They Don't Teach You in Harvard Business School*. In 1979, Harvard MBA students were asked if they had written down their goals. Of the graduating class, 84 percent had no specific goals, and only 13 percent indicated they had specific goals. Only 3 percent of the graduates responded that they had specific goals and had written them down.

Ten years later, the students were asked follow-up questions about earnings and other career-related matters. The results still resonate today. The students who had goals but who hadn't written them down were making twice as much money as the 84 percent of students who had no goals at all. The 3 percent of students who had specific goals and had written them down in 1979 were earning ten times as much as the rest of their peers. These students regularly updated their action plans, and they were self-aware enough to know that goals and plans change over time.

As you practice your ART, not all the feedback you receive will be positive, but I would urge you to keep an open mind. Remember, you are not seeking praise. You are looking to identify blind spots and learn more about how you are perceived. Determining and increasing self-awareness should be a lifelong and routine process, so you can stay on point and on course as an effective leader and manager.

Habitual self-awareness

> Observe all men; thy self most.
> —Benjamin Franklin

Developing self-awareness is a human behavior—one that can and should be cultivated. As human beings, we judge, and we are judged. And we should be aware of how we appear because, whether we like it or not, we are often judged on even the most superficial things, including how we look, what we wear, what we drive, and even the people who surround us. As silly as it may sound, there is a powerful beam of good news here, because superficial things are easily changed.

I have the distinct pleasure of working with Don, an exceptional executive. Don is a good leader and a kind man and is regarded as the gold standard of managers among executives at his software company.

To put it kindly, however, Don's executive assistant was a disaster. Where Don is warm, effusive, and polite, the assistant spoke down to people and was unkind and rude. She represented Don but seemed to have none of the remarkable—and self-aware—qualities of her boss. Indeed, her working style was the antithesis of Don's. True, people have different styles, and Don was the manager, not his assistant, so why am I drilling this point home? Because the assistant's behavior reflected on Don. Albeit not deliberately, she was undermining his image, his brand.

After some months, Don became sufficiently self-aware that his assistant's actions could be his undoing. I am reminded of how parents often tell their preteen and teenage children, "You are who you hang out with." The same was true for Don. As he recognized the detrimental effects that his assistant had on the rest of the team, Don had the self-awareness to conclude that he could no longer "hang out" with her. To sustain his own leadership effectiveness, Don had to let her go.

To be clear, self-awareness is not about being shallow. Self-awareness is not about hanging out with the cool (successful, popular) kids. Self-awareness does, however, require you to pay attention to the people you choose to surround you. The point is not to run with the powerful and to hobnob with the successful. The point is to be aware of what you are projecting. Or, to put it somewhat differently, what you are *protecting*. You are protecting your brand, your image, your reputation. Everything matters. And it can matter in the most unexpected of circumstances.

I once worked with Gail, a humble, fit, and attractive executive. Gail was a midlevel manager who was likely somewhat underpaid and dressed accordingly. Senior managers wanted to groom her for advancement, but time and time again, Gail was passed over for promotions. Was Gail qualified? Yes. Was she deserving? Without a doubt. But still, something was holding her back, and no one seemed quite able to put their finger on it until a series of 360-degree interviews revealed that Gail, among other necessary changes, needed to update her wardrobe. More precisely, a male colleague noted that she needed "a manicure and the name of a good seamstress."

Gail could not have been more surprised at this feedback. Yes, she knew she'd been frugal and that she hadn't paid much attention to her attire. But she was smart and hardworking. She didn't think her appearance was even noticed, much less judged.

In the aftermath, though, Gail made a few changes. She didn't go overboard, of course. She remained true to herself, dressing conservatively and affordably, but she made more of an effort. She made sure her clothes fit properly. She carried herself differently. She deliberately began seeing herself as an executive and began outfitting herself accordingly. She chose to look like a successful leader, and before long, she was seen as one, as well.

These material changes—although simple—can also be the most dramatic. When I took on a leadership role in a company, I was a very practical person. For me, shoes and cars and handbags were for comfort and function, nothing else. I'll never forget the day, though, that I wore a new pair of expensive shoes to work. I'd purchased them on sale and almost instantly regretted the decision. However, the purchase was a final sale. So despite my buyer's remorse, they were mine for keeps—and they were comfortable, to boot!

I wore them to work the next day, and much to my surprise, before I even got to my desk, someone commented on my shoes. No one had ever commented on my footwear before. In fact, as soon as I stepped on the elevator, a person I barely knew said, "I love your shoes!" It was a wake-up call for me. People notice your behavior. They notice the people with whom you surround yourself, and they notice what you look like on a daily basis. Because you are a leader.

Successful leaders have to have a clear view of themselves. They have to be able to project where they want to be and then behave accordingly. Shoes, wardrobe, accessories, and even cars play into this. Argue as you may, that is the world in which we live.

Personally, I hate the idea of "keeping up" with anybody—coworkers, neighbors, or friends. However, I'm keenly aware that we all are judged. There are norms, and there are expectations. If we aren't aware of them or if we choose to ignore them, then we are only doing ourselves damage.

Hyperactive self-awareness

> Know yourself. Don't accept your dog's admiration
> as conclusive evidence that you are wonderful.
> —Ann Landers

As you might expect, too much self-awareness can be every bit as detrimental as too little self-awareness.

Some leaders spend so much time trying to understand how they're perceived that they lose focus. No one—colleagues, peers, family members—wants to be in the position of having to constantly reassure insecure leaders.

Too much self-awareness can make you paranoid. I remind leaders who verge on too much self-awareness that *worrying* about what people think can pull them down. The behavior we're looking for is awareness, not worry. If you're in a meeting and are worried about what people are thinking or what you are wearing, then you can't focus. You have to filter your awareness.

Remember Mike, whom I mentioned at the beginning of the chapter? One of his behavioral solutions was simple. It turned out that his military posture, the one he worked so hard to maintain, was a behavior that was holding him back. It wasn't a problem with his coworkers who knew him well, but the important constituents who didn't work with him on a daily basis—including board members and longtime clients—perceived him as haughty and arrogant. Plainly put, they judged the book by his cover. They thought Mike was arrogant because he held his head high.

My advice could not have been simpler. I asked him to lower his chin.

No kidding. Problem solved.

Leadership roundup

Self-awareness is the first step in identifying ways your behavior might adversely impact your company. Introspection and openness to change go hand in hand with self-awareness. Often, feedback is needed to enhance your ability to be more aware of negative behavior, but the process always starts with you.

- You might think that self-awareness simply means that you understand your emotions, know your strengths and weaknesses, and know what triggers you in situations where you might lose your patience. But this is only half the equation. The second half involves understanding how your behavior impacts your followers and knowing that you can change any negatives as long as you know what they are.
- If you aren't self-aware in both ways, your company will suffer financially. Identify your blind spots by asking for feedback.
- Make a habit of being self-aware. The behavior will become second nature.

- Be aware of how those you work with or those who report to you are perceived. If your team is viewed as positive, you will be too, simply through association. Negative perceptions will have the opposite impact.
- Embrace the ART approach. Ask questions, reach out, and take action. Write an action plan to help you pinpoint which behaviors need work and how you intend to meet the challenge.

Chapter 3

Self-Control

The first and best victory is to conquer self.
—Plato

A friend of mine once had a boss, Max, with a commanding management style. Max barked orders, issued mandates, and set the bar absurdly high. On the rare occasion that an ambitious teammate managed to clear the bar, Max reset it ridiculously higher. Bombastic and demanding, Max was even better known for his volatility and temper. In a morning staff meeting, he might behave as if a teammate were his dearest friend. The same afternoon, Max might turn on that same teammate, verbally humiliating him or her in front of the team. Max did not discriminate. His reputation for unchecked behavior was well earned on all fronts, including teammates and vendors and even clients. Once, while forcefully making a point in a business meeting, Max pounded his fist on the conference table so violently that he required medical attention.

As you'd expect, coworkers, especially his direct reports, didn't just fear Max: they came to hate him. Even those who weren't subjected to his daily wrath found that working with Max sapped their energy and productivity. Frontline colleagues and behind-the-scenes teammates alike were weary before the day even began. The result? Just as you'd expect—and hardly what a leader would want: everyone avoided contact with Max. They dodged meetings with him and carefully constructed e-mails to him so as not to rouse his ire. During the roughest patches, the team spent more time managing their tenuous employment situations than actual work. My friend, usually positive and upbeat, found himself in the unusual position of having to psych himself up each morning before crossing the office threshold and beginning the day.

Max lacked an essential attribute of successful leaders—*self-control*. His overbearing leadership style, atrocious as it was, might have been somewhat successful in a military situation—after all, in a war zone, troops must follow orders in a crisis without question or discussion—but in a traditional workplace, there must be some give-and-take between leaders and followers. Leaders ought to feel respected but so must followers.

The control Max so desperately sought through his brusque tone and forceful actions eluded him because to have control as a leader, he first must *be* in control—of *himself*. As I'm sure you can imagine, Max wasn't the most self-aware guy on the block. In fact, he lacked the first of the core concepts of behavior-based executive leadership techniques. Self-awareness may have led him to wonder if he was doing more harm to his business than good with his overbearing manner. If you kick a dog enough times, it's going to bite you. In Max's case, the "bites" were manifesting themselves in subtle ways. There were no obvious teeth marks, no blood, no torn clothes. But the damage was done anyway.

Self-awareness is obviously the first step in becoming a better leader. If you're self-aware, you will likely have more self-control than a person as clueless as Max. One concept, or behavior, builds on the next, until you have a suite of positive behaviors that trickle down into everything you do every day in your company. Your followers may not be privy to the degree of your self-awareness. Self-awareness is by necessity a private matter. However, when it comes to self-control, you're definitely in the proverbial fishbowl. If you lose it, everybody will know—in minutes, if not seconds!

Self-control positives

> I cannot trust a man to control others
> who cannot control himself.
> —Robert E. Lee

Self-control requires controlling or redirecting one's disruptive impulses and moods. Self-control means suspending judgment and thinking before acting. More than a pleasantry or merely civilized behavior, self-control, in the appropriate measure, is essential to workplace success. Its importance on the list of desirable leadership behaviors cannot be overstated. Indeed, in *The Willpower Instinct*, Kelly McGonigal writes, "Self-control is a better predictor of academic success than intelligence, a stronger determinant of effective leadership than charisma, and more important for marital bliss than empathy."

So why might self-control prove even more valuable to leaders than intelligence, charisma, or empathy? Because a leader's self-control sets a tone for everyone in the workplace and can influence productivity. Moodiness, emotional immaturity, and erratic behavior among managers lead to chaos. And such behaviors are costly too. Volatility in a leader leads to a loss of productivity, as followers squander time and negative energy constantly evaluating and readjusting to an unpredictable and often fearful environment.

For better *and* for worse, a leader leads in a fishbowl. There is no place to hide, as colleagues and direct reports observe—and judge—every move. It is therefore incumbent on a leader to exercise control over his or her words, actions, and even emotions.

I once worked with Edward, the division head of a $500-million service organization. In my initial 360-degree interviews, his team members' reviews were positive. His direct reports expressed awe and respect for Edward's passion for business and entrepreneurship. Eventually, though, it was revealed across the board that, when it came to leadership style, the question du jour was "Did Edward take his meds today?"

To be clear, Edward was not on any medication. He was, however, moody and unpredictable. Unknown to his colleagues, Edward was facing issues in his personal life, and he brought these emotions with him to work because, as a person in power, he felt free to express his every mood. No one had ever explained to him that, on the contrary, as a person in power, he was obligated to abandon the freedom of showing *every* emotion.

Unrestrained emotion is not a leadership perk and in fact can be detrimental not just to the psyches of workers but also to office productivity. Working for an emotional leader like Edward can leave workers feeling like double agents, behaving in front of the leader as if everything is fine and normal but then colluding with colleagues to muddle through the day and tackle the chores at hand, the most important of which is *not* to be productive but instead to maintain individual sanity.

In *Great by Choice,* Jim Collins and Morten Hansen say, "The best leaders have 'fanatic discipline.'" I would be the first to agree with what you may be thinking: "fanatic discipline" can be something of a burden. But I also know that climbing the ladder or staying at the top requires relinquishing a few privileges. People are watching how you act. They're reacting to what you say, and they're deciding, *Do I or do I not want to follow this person?*

Would my team be willing to follow me over a hill? It's a question every leader must ask, because following is an individual choice, not a managerial mandate. While insufficient self-control in a leader can lead to chaos, abundant and appropriate self-control can inspire confidence. Self-restraint creates a healthy environment where team members feel comfortable taking risks. Self-discipline fosters a productive work environment where employees feel valued and important. Self-regulation makes it easy and safe for team members to follow, and without followers, a true and effective leader cannot exist. One might, on an organizational chart, be a "manager," but the very definition of *leader* requires followers, and following defies organizational charts.

Even the best-intentioned leaders can lose self-control. When my daughters were toddlers, my work situation became very stressful. I worked for a highly regarded, high-profile company at the time. I suppose you could say that the position itself was fairly prestigious, but like so many other companies in that decade, ours was awash with corporate layoffs, mergers and acquisitions, and divesture. I reeled from the loss of colleagues and coworkers. As one major US company after the other was going through bankruptcy, I dreaded the possibility of my company's failure. I didn't fear the other shoe dropping; I feared a shoe closet the size of Imelda Marcos's dropping. In one three-year period, I reported to four different bosses. And yet, to my credit—or, perhaps, to my detriment—I kept my emotions in check. I'd always prided myself on self-control at work and maintained a stalwart facade. I would never be one of those people who cried on the job. The stress, however, was undeniable. Yes, I could maintain tight control at work, but I couldn't erase it. I ended up carrying my stress home, only to reveal it to the people I loved most—my supportive husband and my sweet baby girls.

I was lucky, though. Before too long, my own mother pulled me aside and gave me a firm talking-to. She knew—and I quickly agreed—that I was wrong and out of line. If I didn't make some changes, she knew (correctly) that I'd have regrets. In a way, Mom was *my* leadership coach. She pointed out the error of my ways and turned me around.

Moral licensing

> Rank does not confer privilege or give power.
> It imposes responsibility.
> —Peter F. Drucker

As essential as self-control is to effective leadership, experts agree that lapses in self-control are a pervasive problem among executives. As leaders acquire responsibility and power, many give themselves "permission" to lose control. This idea is commonly called *moral licensing*, a term in social psychology describing when people allow themselves to indulge after doing something positive. It is similar to that of a zealous dieter who scrimps on every calorie, works out maniacally, and then splurges on a chocolate sundae.

Sadly, for the splurging manager, the results are similar to the dieter. The loss of control negates the earlier good management behaviors. Plain and simple, moral licensing is tantamount to self-sabotage. A leader might rationalize his or her uncontrolled behavior, believing that good deeds erase the repercussions of inappropriate behavior, but this is incorrect thinking.

As Kelly McGonigal, author of *The Willpower Instinct*, explains, moral licensing can slip up on a person: "When you do something good, you feel good about yourself. This means you're more likely to trust your impulses—which means give yourself permission to do something bad."

Consider the example of Jake, a CEO who is extraordinarily generous with compensation and perks and benefits for his employees. Jake's policies are also remarkably considerate of employees' families and loved ones. You might expect, then, that his employees would feel grateful, and to an extent, they do. However, they also feel handcuffed, because in day-to-day dealings, Jake is an out-of-control manager. He is the proverbial bull in a china shop—except the china shop is his own company. Employees walk on eggshells around him, afraid to make waves. They fear for their jobs. They fear losing all those over-the-top benefits. They fear taking risks, which ultimately means that they fear doing their jobs in the best way possible. Jake has sabotaged his good intentions—and indeed, the entire company—with his bad behavior. His Jekyll-and-Hyde behavior has caused the people in his company to develop a love-hate relationship with him.

Jake will boast about contributing to the educational fund of a needy employee's family and taking care of another's exorbitant medical bills. He is sincere and earnest in his intentions and actions, earning gratitude and loyalty. But then, Jake will unexpectedly erupt for a small reason in the workplace and talk down to the same employees, treating them disrespectfully, never stopping to think about his own inconsistent behavior.

Moral licensing can also be detrimental to leaders who are too self-controlled. Leaders who do all the right things at work, leaders who tightly control their emotions in the office, and leaders who, by the nature of the job itself, have no margin for error at work can feel so controlled that they grant themselves permission to blow a gasket—that is, lose control—elsewhere. The leader who is stalwart at work might be utterly unpredictable at home or perhaps unpredictable in secretive and harmful ways at work.

Again, it all comes back to self-control. And you can't have full self-control without a highly developed sense of self-awareness.

The three-second rule

> You can tell the size of a man
> by the size of the thing that makes him mad.
> —Adlai Stevenson

Allowing oneself to lose control in a business environment is an archaic style of leadership. Still, in my experience, most leaders with self-control issues are good people at heart. Often, the solution to many self-control issues is pretty simple. I like to call it the three-second rule. Essentially, it's a variation of counting to ten before you blow your stack or taking a deep breath before you hit send on that acerbic or sarcastic e-mail you just wrote to your boss. If you're self-aware, you'll know you're about to lose it. So stop and tell yourself to calm down. Don't give yourself permission to dive off the deep end.

Let's take a look at two of my clients who had some self-control challenges. The first one we'll name John. He was a surgeon who saw himself as direct and honest. He thought he was self-aware, but he didn't have the benefit of a good feedback loop to assist him in obtaining a truly accurate assessment of how others perceived him. Colleagues regarded him as intimidating and dismissive. Well before our paths crossed, I'd heard tales of his surgical brilliance. Highly regarded physicians wanted to work alongside him. Impressionable medical school students wanted to emulate him. Desperate patients lined up to receive his expertise and care. John's operating room prowess was legendary, and sadly, so was his uncontrollable temper.

Being strident, judgmental, and vociferous had served John well as he'd climbed the ranks from medical student to successful surgeon. Once established as a leader in the field, though, John was ill served by these same qualifications. He didn't recognize it, of course, but even from an outsider's perspective, the evidence was undeniable. Colleagues were united in their fear of waking the beast. Associates went well out of their way to avoid confrontation. Many avoided contact with him altogether. Still, John thought everything was fine, that he was at the top of his game professionally, and he was. The problem was he was a fiend to work with, and that was planting land mines that could threaten his future despite his brilliance.

John was genuinely confounded when, after a series of 360-degree interviews with his colleagues, I shared that his lack of self-control was an issue. What was obvious to everyone else came as a shock to John. From his perspective, he was only "making a point." And since he was "right," he had no reason to suffer fools gladly. Pressed further, he would insist that he was saving his coworkers time. By asserting the truth (as he saw it) with surgical precision, if you will, John believed that he was saving others from wasting time—theirs and his—as they stuttered and stumbled their way to what would surely be, in John's eyes, the "wrong" conclusion.

To his credit, though, John earnestly wanted to correct the situation and was willing to change his behavior. Although he did not actually understand his colleagues' perspective, he realized that his lack of control was a problem that put his career in jeopardy. His desire to correct the situation led me to suggest a simple first step. I gave him the three-second rule, asking him to pause for at *least* three seconds before responding to, criticizing, or interrupting a colleague or patient.

The idea was twofold. First, simply by letting another person speak his or her piece and complete a thought, John was exercising some self-control. Second, by putting his own thoughts aside—even if for only three seconds—John was validating the speaker, thus inspiring confidence in John as a leader. And there was a side benefit: not only did the speaker feel valued, but also John was surprised to realize that many of his colleagues and associates actually had valuable contributions to make. Indeed, John was so pleased with the results of the three-second rule that he began applying it outside of work—at home and with friends—with similar satisfying results.

Another executive, Margi, was a director in a $400-million global manufacturing company, on track to become controller and eventually CFO. The one thing that seemed to be holding her back was her lack of self-restraint, so the president of the company asked me to step in. Many coworkers pointed out, "She doesn't have a filter," and Margi's 360-degree feedback and behavioral/EQ assessment confirmed that she indeed did not hold back her thoughts. In short, she was another prime candidate for the three-second rule.

From what I heard, Margi made no effort to hide her thoughts and feelings. If she was exasperated with an individual or in a meeting, she blatantly smirked or made snide, hurtful comments. Sometimes she was uncaring, and other times she was completely unaware of how the targets of her wrath took her words or behavior.

When I initially gave Margi the 360-degree feedback from her colleagues, she admitted that her behavior was not always completely professional. But she had no idea how badly she was alienating her colleagues. As I shared more and more feedback, Margi became embarrassed by the way she was coming across. As a fast-tracked senior manager, she did not want to come across as childish. Among other things, I suggested that she work on enhancing her self-awareness, as I knew that if she was more in touch with herself, she'd be more likely to realize when she was sauntering toward the no-man's-land of losing her cookies. Next, I pointed out that self-control often requires simply the soundness of mind to stop and think. The three-second rule really does work. It did for John and Margi.

Childish is how employees commonly describe managers with low self-control. Like little children, these managers blurt out anything on their minds without thinking. In the same vein, colleagues said that John, the brilliant surgeon, "acted like a sixteen-year-old" and had "no filter."

If you are a leader, you cannot let other people see how you are feeling every day. You have tremendous impact on other people's moods. Imagine, the whole company, the whole organization, going up and down with you and your moods. You cannot afford that. Yes, there is a time and place for letting your guard down and confiding your vulnerabilities—but only with the right people at the right time and in a controlled manner.

Margi needed a plan. More than working on specific behaviors and learning to anticipate their eruption, we also had to focus on controlling Margi's body language and words. The road was rocky. As with so many leaders, Margi's behaviors were ingrained. She struggled to make changes, so I gave her an assignment, asking her to pretend that one of her direct reports was the one with low self-restraint and that she was that person's coach. She then made a list of dos and don'ts for meeting behaviors. This list—the one made for "someone else"—was the one Margi began referring to during her own meetings.

As Margi herself reports, "I have learned to choose the right words and anticipate their impact. In the past, I spoke without thinking, but I am now getting more comfortable with pausing and collecting my thoughts before I speak."

Margi has even become aware of her body language. Once, her facial expressions were as easily read as an open book. "I breathe now," she explains, and "when necessary, if something makes me angry, I pretend it's funny."

It's not always easy or automatic, though. In some cases, when leaders aren't sure of how to respond or behave themselves, I encourage them to think of someone else who behaves with dignity and self-restraint. In Margi's case, she chose to think of the president of the organization, Jack. "If I'm under real duress, I'll force myself to pause, and I'll ask myself, 'What would Jack do? How would he behave?'"

For Margi, the difference has been absolute and undeniable. Six months later, I held discussions with the same 360-degree respondents as before. The improvement was obvious, and Margi was rewarded with a promotion.

The WAIT principle

> Self-reverence, self-knowledge, self-control;
> these three alone lead one to sovereign power.
> —Alfred Lord Tennyson

Have you ever replied to an e-mail in a fit of rage or self-righteousness? Perhaps a colleague sent you an e-mail that made your blood boil, and, by God, you were going to give him or her a piece of your mind. And not just this one colleague, because in your rush to react, you chose to Reply All and put this know-it-all in his or her place.

And then, *boom!*

No, that wasn't you hitting a target; that was you backfiring. You could have avoided the embarrassment, or even potential termination, if you'd adhered to the three-second rule. However, sometimes that rule isn't enough. You need more. That's why you should also be familiar with the WAIT principle. Just what is it? The WAIT principle is shorthand for a very useful question: Why am I talking? If you ask yourself this question before you jump right in with an opinion or comment, you are applying the WAIT principle to your behavior in the workplace. In essence, you're giving yourself the chance to be self-aware enough to exercise the self-control you need to be the best possible leader.

Here are some questions that help sum up the WAIT principle:

Why. Am I talking to make myself feel good about myself? Am I talking to impress someone else? Am I talking to deny someone else's good idea? Is this something a good and effective leader would do?

Am. Am I too engrossed in the moment? What am I trying to be? Who am I trying to be?

I. Who is this about? Is it even about me? Should I be deferring to someone else in this conversation or specific moment?

Talking. Am I saying one thing with my body and something different with my words? What is my body language projecting at the moment? What is my facial expression saying? Do I really need to talk?

The best and most-mature leaders understand the importance of cadence, or timing. Their mastery of self-control includes an incredible sense of pace and rhythm. They know when to time a counterpoint to a conversation in a meeting, when to exhibit anger, when to send an off-putting e-mail, and when to keep their fingers off the Send button.

By far, the biggest struggle in self-control is *timing*. Those with too little self-control need to slow down. Those with too much may need to hit the fast-forward button. Generally speaking, the former is the most common problem with many leaders. Far fewer suffer from too much self-control. The reason for this is pretty simple. At the risk of speaking in too broad a generality, most leaders are type A personalities. These individuals got where they are because they're not about to sit passively by and take what life throws at them. On the contrary, they are ready to get up and go, and if they get knocked down, they're ready to get up and go some more. The three-second rule and the WAIT principle both are meant to tamp down the frequently explosive natures of type A leaders. Timing, with all of its nuances, is at the core of learning (or enhancing) self-control.

Timing and self-control aren't issues exclusive to the business world. Remember the 2006 World Cup final in Berlin when one player head-butted another and got ejected, costing his team the game? Remember the high-ranking American tennis player who threatened a line judge, which resulted in a penalty point that cost her the match? Let's take a look at another case study.

Nicholas, the CEO of a growing $2-billion retail company, told me once that his impulse to fire words and written communications was one of the hardest behaviors for him to control. He said, "I have been rewarded my whole life for going fast and being the first with the correct answer." From elementary school through grad school and even during the first half of his career, he impressed teachers and bosses with his quick wit and speedy solutions. But what happened when he ascended into leadership, guiding many other people? His fiery speed alienated those around him.

For Nicholas, quick thinking was a gift that became a curse. It wasn't a characteristic he needed to eliminate; however, it was something he had to control. He had to learn to differentiate situations when his speed was beneficial versus situations when his speed was, to put it plainly, obnoxious. Although it required a supreme effort, Nicholas had to teach himself to *slow down*—slow down his speaking, slow down his reacting, and even slow down his breathing.

Nicholas learned to apply the WAIT principle to his management style. Before clicking Send, before responding rashly and bluntly, before cutting off a colleague, before making a snap decision, he first slowed down.

In his marshmallow experiment conducted in the 1960s, psychologist Dr. Walter Mischel gave children one marshmallow with the promise of a second marshmallow if the children didn't eat the first until the experimenter returned. Not surprisingly, some children couldn't resist, while others were able to delay gratification in order to receive a second marshmallow.

Here's the thing, though: when Mischel followed up with the test subjects as young adults, he noted clear differences between those who waited and those who did not. Those who had delayed gratification tended to be more intellectually skilled, responsible, dependable, and attentive. They also excelled at forming relationships and self-control in frustrating situations.

Those who couldn't wait tended to be more easily distracted and less dependable as adults. They had lower intellectual abilities and struggled to exercise self-control under pressure.

Personally, I'm not a fan of marshmallows, so the skeptic in me has to question whether the results would have been somewhat different if the treat were chocolate instead. Still, it's curious to consider that impulsivity may begin at an early age and, left uncontrolled, may lead to struggles at work in general and with leadership in specific.

So pause. Control yourself. Apply the WAIT principle to guide your thinking and your words. The WAIT principle is about output. The three-second rule, on the other hand, relates more to your listening abilities. It is more about input. Both depend on timing, and both depend on self-control.

Laid-back leaders

> You have power over your mind, not outside events.
> Realize this, and you will find strength.
> —Marcus Aurelius

Too much self-control can be equally detrimental to effective leadership. Being a strong, effective leader requires making a connection with followers. You have to be able to celebrate good times and share in the inevitable sadness, disappointment, and failure the workplace and individuals experience. In other words, being an effective leader requires being able to loosen the reins a bit.

Leaders who impose too much control on themselves are also likely to fall into the trap of imposing too much control on team members, with predictable and unfortunate results. Tightly controlled workers don't feel useful or valuable. Instead, they feel disempowered and don't develop, which is to say that taking control from your employees ends up backfiring on you, as a leader. Yes, you may temporarily feel satisfied that tasks are being performed *exactly the way you want*, but employees who are too tightly controlled begin losing their sense of priority and worth.

The controlling boss almost always loses money on the bottom line through a lack of employee productivity, the pollution of negativity on morale, and the HR costs incurred due to employee turnover. Most people would rather not work, if possible, especially in the lower levels of a company. A leader should understand that and take steps to create a corporate culture that encourages cooperation, open communication, and the freedom to innovate when appropriate. Departmental competition often results from leaders exerting too much control. Competition of this sort harms productivity and quality control and can actually sabotage client relations. When followers feel diminished in the eyes of an overcontrolling leader, their work suffers, and the overcontrolling leader ends up feeling obligated to take on even more work and feeling even more overwhelmed.

Now picture the complete opposite. The type B or type C leader lets it all hang out. He or she isn't assertive. Employees get all the freedom they need, and supervision and oversight is limited. This sort of corporate culture can work in some cases, but it is risky to encourage. Often, the failure to lead assertively with the right balance arises from the tendency of the leader to exert too much internal self-control. In other words, the leader with too much self-control fails to rock the boat when necessary. As just noted, the right balance and timing is essential for a successful, self-aware leader with the perfect blend of self-control in the corporate arena.

I once had the pleasure of working with Mary, a perfectly polished and professional executive. Clients and coworkers alike saw her as always able to get the job done. No hurdle was too high and no deadline too pressing. Mary could always deliver. Equally impressive was the way she went about her work. She never complained or seemed uncertain about the fast track she embraced. She never showed negative emotions or flinched in the face of impossible tasks. She was like that duck that seemed to be gliding effortlessly across a pond but, in fact, was furiously paddling below the surface.

But who could tell? No one. Indeed, that was the problem. No one could tell. Since Mary kept such a tight rein on her emotions and personal life, neither senior executives nor coworkers had any idea of how Mary was feeling as a human being. While they could admire her as a professional, teammates had problems relating to her. She showed no vulnerability.

As she'd climbed the management ladder, this get-it-done work style had worked for Mary. Who could complain about an employee who could get every job done—perfectly—virtually every time? As a leader, however, Mary eventually found this tactic to be ineffective. Her tightly controlled behavior, though superficially effective in accomplishing tasks and pleasing clients, made it difficult for her to attract followers. She appeared efficient, even laid-back, but she was not in a good place. She just had to admit it to herself. Eventually, she did.

Ironically, Mary saw this perceived lack of vulnerability as a strength. She took pride in the fact that no one knew when she was stressed out or insecure. Colleagues and direct reports called her superwoman, which may have seemed flattering but in fact resulted in negative perceptions, such as "We can never be like her," "Who in real life can be like superwoman?" and "She's perfect—I can't measure up."

I suggested that Mary begin sharing—selectively—her work-related emotions. Initially, the idea was intimidating. Mary was understandably concerned that letting colleagues or direct reports know when she was nervous, anxious, or insecure would cause them to lose their respect— that it would be an admission of her weaknesses. I argued, though, that showing no emotion can be interpreted as having no passion. Which is all to say that too much self-control can backfire.

A leader with too much self-control can be seen as robotic and unfeeling. Where a leader with too little control can be seen as a bull in a china shop, a leader with too much control risks being perceived as a zombie. Effective leaders have to find the balance. We all have flaws. We all have chinks in our armor, cracks in the veneer. And these are the things that make us human and accessible. And this is attractive to our fellow human beings.

When Hillary Clinton campaigned for US president in 2008, she was regarded as one tough cookie. Poised and confident, she hadn't cracked during the many years of media scrutiny. She rarely even cracked a smile. Even during the time of her husband's indiscretion, Hillary had remained—at least in front of reporters—calm, cool, and collected. Talk about self-controlled! As it turns out, though, even Hillary had a chink in her armor. Years later, on Hillary's campaign trail, a well-intentioned voter asked a weary and worn Hillary an innocent question: "How do you do it? How do you keep up?"

And the veneer cracked. Hillary's eyes welled up, and she fought back tears as she responded emotionally about the challenges of campaigning for political office. She showed vulnerability. And suddenly, voters perceived her differently. Poll numbers surged, and Hillary unexpectedly snatched a last-minute New Hampshire primary win over her challenger, Barack Obama. Perhaps Hillary showed her human side earnestly and impulsively that day. Or perhaps she listened to an adviser's or coach's advice to display some emotion. Whichever it was, it worked.

On another political front, much hay was made when President George W. Bush, who was visiting an elementary school classroom at the time, showed virtually no reaction upon hearing the whispered news of planes crashing into the World Trade Center on 9/11. He was accused of having too much self-control, of showing too little emotion, too little reaction. I'd have to ask, though, what would have happened if he had reacted strongly, emotionally, or even violently? What if he had lost it? How would he have been perceived? By the young students in front of him? By the victims? By citizens? By international leaders? In this instance, I'd say if the president erred, it was on the side of caution, which, given the circumstances, was appropriate and even admirable.

Self-control is desirable, to be sure, but it requires balance. Nobody wants to work with, or for, a robot.

Profanity

> Profanity is the effort of a feeble brain to express itself forcibly.
> —Spencer W. Kimball

My advice about profanity? *Don't use it.* The risk is too high. The potential benefits, short-lived.

I know. All the cool kids do it. But consider this one example. Carol Bartz, a hard-driving, fearless leader and former CEO of Yahoo, relied on salty language to help level the testosterone-laden playing field. After losing her job, she had one regret. "I probably wouldn't have said the F-word."

Research indicates that cursing is the number-one reason employees get fired. According to a survey conducted by TheLadders.com, an online provider of senior talent, more than 80 percent of executives believe that cursing is inappropriate in the workplace. Most, in fact, say that profanity is grounds for termination.

Consider another perspective. A friend's college daughter earned a remarkable internship in the precise medical discipline of her choice. The daughter beamed with pride when she told me of this honor, and my friend beamed with pride as he shared the news with friends, family, and colleagues. Before long, though, the daughter's confidence in her mentors was rattled as she witnessed their coarse and inappropriate language. She'd heard rough language before but never in a workplace and certainly not the type of profanity that might wilt the ears of the saltiest sailor.

In almost every circumstance, profanity cheapens the speaker. Profane words merely suffice when the speaker is unable to come up with the best word for a situation. So yes, using profanity can make the speaker seem uneducated and inarticulate. Moreover, the risk of offending other people is too high. Although the offended person will likely not confront you, the repercussions can be long lasting, reaching far beyond a human resource department's ability to resolve.

Remember when the rapper Kanye West made such a scene during the 2009 Video Music Awards? He rudely interrupted country singer Taylor Swift's acceptance speech, snatching the microphone to share his opinion that Ms. Swift wasn't the rightful, worthy award recipient.

Shocking? Yes. But even more shocking was that the president of the United States, Barack Obama, weighed in a few days later, referring (off the record) to Kanye as a "jackass."

Truth? Perhaps. But appropriate for the leader of the free world? Perhaps not. Even off the record, the potential downside was too great. The president's remark became the comment heard round the world. Rather than seeming hip or cool, President Obama lost his opportunity to stand on the high ground.

To be truthful, I have no quantitative evidence that the use of swear words always undermines leadership. And I'll even admit that there may be a place for profanity in your life. Certain work environments— trading floors, operating rooms, locker rooms—seem to actually encourage the use of profane language. In these situations, there may be a prevailing sense that playing the profanity card is necessary to ascend the hierarchy. Even so, being a leader doesn't mean doing what everyone else is doing. One should question the value of achieving "success" by behaving poorly. An effective leader must question what communication is achieved through swearing. Are you storytelling, joking, managing stress, expressing aggression, trying to fit in? Does swearing really communicate what you think it does?

In most work environments, there's no call for a leader to lean on the crutch of profanity. Employees, and perhaps customers and onlookers, consider you a corporate role model; others watch and want to emulate your choices. Look around. The best leaders control their profanity. Would you prefer to be seen as dignified or profane?

Listen to yourself. Control yourself. *Represent* yourself.

Mastering self-control

> May I ever practice self-control,
> May I learn to be patient and kind;
> May I meet my problems with wisdom;
> If I do, I will have peace of mind.
> —Gertrude Tooley Buckingham

Mastering self-control comes from self-awareness. As I've said, if you are self-aware, you'll realize that you may need to address self-control challenges as you refine your personal leadership style in the context of behavior-based action plans. The problem is that you may not know that self-control issues exist even if you are growing in terms of your own self-awareness. That's why feedback is so important. Others see you the way they see you, and that's not necessarily how you see yourself. Feedback is that mirror I've spoken of. Sometimes you'll find a reflection that's completely different from what you expected to see.

If you're seen as a control freak, type A boss, understand that you need to take steps to master the right balance of self-control. The three-second rule will help you give others the chance to voice their opinions; some of the input you receive may be excellent. The three-second rule will also stop you (hopefully) from putting your foot in your mouth.

Likewise, the WAIT principle will prompt you to ask a series of questions before you assert yourself. These questions enhance self-awareness. Self-awareness and self-control lead to better communication between you and your followers.

And if you are overly controlling of your own emotions, understand that a balance between being assertive and laid-back (even if you're not feeling laid-back) is the key to enhancing your overall standing as a leader. Either way, improving as a leader is a good thing. Your employees will be happier, and so will you. Productivity and profits are likely to increase.

Leadership roundup

Self-control is the second essential component of a behavior-based approach to leadership. Nothing will undermine you more than losing it in front of your followers. The problem is many leaders don't know that others see them as over the top or even as childish because of outbursts, aggression in the workplace, or aloofness that's taken as insensitivity or arrogance. As with self-awareness, feedback is important as you go about identifying your blind spots in this area. The good news is that leaders who have both self-awareness and self-control are poised to achieve stellar success not only for themselves on a personal level but also for the companies they lead.

- Be wary of moral licensing—giving yourself permission to blow off steam just because you feel you've earned the right.
- The views of your teammates matter, as do those of your direct reports. If you have the tendency to jump right in to save time or because you think you know better, try the three-second rule. You may be pleased with the positive results.
- Before interrupting a subordinate, apply the WAIT principle—ask yourself, "Why am I talking?" Similar to the three-second rule, the WAIT principle will help you pause and regain self-control.
- Avoid profanity. Swearing, even in a casual way, makes you look bad as a leader. Good leaders express themselves without the use of profanity.
- Too much self-control can give the impression that you are laid-back and don't care about running a tight ship. Productivity may suffer. Likewise, if you bottle things up because you feel you always need to be totally self-controlling, you could create stress you might not otherwise have. Balance is required.

Chapter 4

Empathy

When you show deep empathy toward others,
their defensive energy goes down, and positive energy replaces it.
That's when you can get more creative in solving problems.
—Stephen Covey

Richard, a fast-track executive quickly ascending the ranks of an international consulting company, was clearly being groomed by senior management for bigger and better things when my services were requested to move things along. I wasn't entirely clear, though, why I was being brought in. Richard was his company's golden boy; I could see that he was highly regarded. The two of us hit it off immediately. Where other executives often resist the very notion of leadership coaching, Richard embraced it. He was a quick study, keenly interested in doing whatever it takes and eager to lead and inspire his followers.

Given his receptiveness, I was certain he'd be just as eager to act upon some of the verbatim feedback I'd gathered from colleagues and subordinates during my routine 360-degree interviews about him. However, I couldn't have been farther from the mark. "I'm sorry, Paulette," he blurted out, "but I'm not really interested in these people or what they think."

Wow. Let me say that again. *Wow.* I did not see that one coming. The golden boy's Achilles' heel was his lack of empathy.

Empathy defined

> Empathy is about finding echoes of another person in yourself.
> —Mohsin Hamid

Often confused with *sympathy* or *compassion*, *empathy* is the ability to understand the emotional makeup, thoughts, and behaviors of other people. Unlike sympathy or compassion, the key to empathy is *understanding*—understanding with detachment, which is far more easily said than done. Empathy is about understanding other people's thoughts, emotions, and behaviors. At its root, the understanding I am talking about must sprout from a finely honed sense of self-awareness. Without being aware of your own feelings, thoughts, desires, hopes, stressors, and triggers, you can't possibly understand how your followers might perceive you. You also won't be able to understand your followers in a way that will help you lead them to full productivity and efficiency.

For a leader, empathy is essential. When you can understand and predict behaviors, you can influence thoughts and decisions. If you can do that in the workplace, imagine how successful your organization—and you—can become.

Empathy is not a moral option in the workplace; it is an absolute necessity. Think about how much more smoothly your office would operate if you truly understood your coworkers. Think how much more efficient you might be if—from the very beginning of the recruiting and hiring process—you could more accurately read prospective employees and identify the ones most likely to have success and longevity in your company.

Conversely, a lack of empathy sets a predictable domino effect into motion. Since Richard was unable to understand the emotional makeup of his colleagues and followers, he was unable to lead effectively. Without understanding people's emotional makeup, he could not understand how they thought. And without understanding how people thought, he could not predict their reactions to his words or behaviors. And since he could not predict their reactions, he could not foresee how his employees would behave. And, well ... you get it.

On a certain level, almost every business executive understands the importance of empathetic behavior. More typically, though, empathetic behavior is directed at customers or consumers, not employees. If you have any doubt, consider the dollars devoted to predicting consumer behavior. Grocery stores, for example, understand which type of background music, at which times of day, on which days of the week, will lead to higher sales in the checkout line. They pay a hefty price to better understand how their shoppers will react and behave, in order to make them linger longer in the produce section, for example, or move more quickly through self-checkout lines. Retailers understand whether potential buyers are more tempted by "50 percent off when you buy two" or "buy two, get one free." They want to understand how buyers will behave. And to understand anyone, one has to be empathetic.

Should there not be just as great an interest in understanding your employees, your coworkers, your board of directors, or your shareholders? In being able to predict what they will think and feel? In leading in a way to maximize productivity and efficiency?

Understanding your followers

> There is only one way ... to get anybody to do anything.
> And that is by making the other person want to do it.
> —Dale Carnegie

Business development and sales require figuring out all your constituencies. Even on a grand scale, companies benefit from understanding both employees and customers. While at the helm of Apple, Steve Jobs may not have been the most empathetic leader, but his products were designed with an intrinsic understanding of consumers. He understood American consumers to the point that he could deliver what consumers themselves didn't even know they needed or wanted. When consumers were overwhelmed with complicated computer manuals and software, Jobs introduced a simple plug-and-play computer. When consumers wanted the ability to carry around their music, he didn't simply create a portable version of a home stereo or boom box; he introduced a new concept—the iPod. And as mobile phones became increasingly complicated, he introduced a phone with just one button, the iPhone. Despite his purported lack of personal empathy for employees, Jobs plainly understood his customer constituency—perhaps even better than they themselves did.

On the other hand, lack of consumer empathy led to one of greatest product fiascoes of all time—New Coke. The company had done its homework, research, and surveys, and all of that indicated that consumers preferred the taste of New Coke. What the company failed to *understand* was how consumers felt about "old" Coke. Consumers simply couldn't make the switch. In fact, they were indignant at the very idea of replacing the Coca-Cola of their childhood. Despite the fancy ads and marketing and science, New Coke never stood a chance.

Whether you are leading a multimillion-dollar company or a weekend volunteer project, your leadership cannot exist without the ability to influence people—whether it's managing up (influencing your bosses, shareholders, or boards of directors), sideways (teammates and coworkers), or downward (your direct reports and departments). So think, for a moment, how many followers you might attract if you could read other people's minds. Think of what you could accomplish if you could align other people to your way of thinking. Consider how effective you could be. Consider what you could achieve.

I'm not speaking, of course, of the evil mustachioed characters of science-fiction movies or the Vulcan mind meld of the original *Star Trek* television series. I'm talking purely and simply about *empathy*. I'm talking about crafting a message to another person, another *individual*, that takes into account that person's motivations, weaknesses, and strengths.

I'm speaking about having a genuine understanding of your people's concerns, mindsets, and priorities. The better a leader understands his or her prospective followers and the more he or she understands that each human being (leaders *and* followers alike) is intrinsically and genetically different, the more a leader can build rapport, gain influence, and, ultimately, achieve predictable *and desirable* outcomes.

Not only did Richard, the fast-track executive, lack empathy, but when this shortcoming was pointed out, he failed to recognize the value of empathetic behavior. He failed to grasp the efficiency and sheer cleverness of leading first by understanding where people are coming from. He failed to understand that a greater understanding of his employees could lead him to getting them to where he wanted them to go.

Using empathy

> When you really listen to another person from their point of view,
> and reflect back to them that understanding,
> it's like giving them emotional oxygen.
> —Stephen Covey

Empathy is not about manipulation. It's not even about emotion. As I often point out, you don't have to like people to understand them, although liking them certainly helps your propensity to understand them. Empathy is about understanding how someone else will react. Once you understand your effect on people (with self-awareness), you can better understand how they'll react.

In other words, developing empathy (and it can indeed be developed) puts you on a path to more easily achieve your personal (and your company's) goals.

Sadly, business leaders have an unfortunate history of falling short when it comes to empathetic behavior. In decades past, I can remember times when security officials escorted laid-off employees from the building. Not only were these employees publicly humiliated, but the workers who remained—the "survivors"—had their own guilt. They were simultaneously relieved, depressed, sad, and entirely unproductive.

Was this what their leaders intended? Certainly not. The thought, almost surely, was that trimming the workforce would make it more productive, not less so. It took quite some time, though, for the culture to change and for organizations to implement not only better strategies for laying off people but also better strategies for managing the survivors. Eventually, leaders and human resources departments realized the need to take care of their remaining employees to make sure they felt secure. They realized that insecure employees could not be productive, which was entirely counter to the original strategy of laying off workers to increase productivity.

In his book *The First 90 Days: Proven Strategies for Getting Up to Speed Faster and Smarter*, Michael D. Watkins provides strategies for conquering the challenges of transitions, whether you are being promoted internally or hired by a board of directors to lead another organization. His key premise? The need for leaders to identify the exact areas—and people—they need to understand. In other words, the need for empathy.

Again, empathy—not sympathy and not manipulation—can move mountains. Another of my clients, Laura, was hired to lead a professional association that was somewhat resistant to the idea of having a new president. It would have been a challenging situation for most leaders, but Laura had always scored high on empathy. A thoughtful and engaging leader, Laura truly understood people's motivations, thoughts, and behaviors. She carried these behaviors with her as she transitioned to her new organization. She was deliberate and methodical and took time to figure out people in groups. Once she understood how to motivate key people, Laura began executing cultural transformation with their buy-in. Unlike so many before her, Laura's transition into her new organization was extremely successful. She did not come in as the new sheriff in town. She came in as an empathetic leader.

And that made all the difference.

I am reminded of Donald, the account supervisor in a marketing organization, who was diligently preparing for the performance review of Bill, one of his account managers. It was Bill's first performance review with the company. He'd been with the company for twelve months, and not only was he failing to meet his goals, but his supervisor, Donald, doubted that the young man was in the right role or even competent. At the most basic level, Donald doubted the young man's future with the company.

Being a straightforward person, Donald explained it to me bluntly: "There's no easy way to do this. Bill has to change. He's not getting the job done. I am just going to give him his review, show him where he failed, and tell him he needs to meet these goals in the next quarter."

Was Donald being honest? Yes. Some might even say brutally so. But remember, his real goal wasn't to be honest. His real goal was to get Bill to meet his quarterly goals. So would Donald's approach work? Probably not. Donald was thinking only of what he wanted, not how he could influence Bill to make the needed changes. Donald had no idea how Bill would respond to the negative review, much less what he could do to change Bill's behavior.

Empathy requires putting ourselves into someone else's brain, seeing things the way he or she does, and even, on occasion, putting ourselves into someone else's shoes, if only temporarily.

When I started my career as a management trainee at a large power company, I was required to spend weeks at a time in a series of nonmanagement roles. Did I have a gift for digging ditches or reading meters or riding in bucket trucks or answering customer calls? Hardly.

But my employer had the right idea. Consider how much more influence I might have when I had a solid understanding of individual employees and the work they performed. This is precisely why so many organizations encourage cross-functional training and assignments.

The television series *Undercover Boss* has turned this very premise into a popular reality show. In each episode, the president or CEO of a well-known company with many locations travels incognito to tackle jobs in various departments. Tantalized viewers tune in as high-ranking executives clean out septic tanks and make meatball sandwiches.

The voyeurs among us may take special delight in seeing these white-collar execs humble themselves, struggling to accomplish what they previously considered to be simple and menial tasks. As a behaviorist, however, I think the bigger lessons are the ones the execs learn from the workers themselves, who have no idea that they are interacting with, and often instructing, their boss. Inevitably, the bosses learn—usually the hard way—to put themselves into their workers' brains, to understand their motivations. On occasion, the bosses are even pleasantly surprised to learn that workers' concerns and happiness hinge on programs already in place or actions that can be easily taken to resolve issues.

The problem with so many of us when it comes to understanding other people and having empathy is remembering that it is *not* about us. Other people do not think the way we do, which means that they will not necessarily react the way we would to certain situations. We don't have to like the person to understand that. We just have to be self-aware enough to realize the reality of most human interactions and then behave in a way that takes the predicted reaction into account.

I asked Donald to imagine what would be going through Bill's mind as he received the negative feedback. He answered, "Well, if it were *me*, I would be embarrassed, and I would know exactly what to do, and I would tell my boss I'm going to do it."

Donald isn't Bill, of course. Therein lies the problem. I cannot tell you how many times I've heard leaders say about their direct reports, "If it were me …" I typically respond, "It's not you. That's why you're the boss." And on the other hand, when I am coaching individual contributors, I try to teach them to think like their leaders. Conversely, my advice to them is to try to understand what is in their leader's mind and to adapt and, if appropriate, to mimic the leader's behavior.

The Platinum Rule

Do not do unto others as you would that they should do unto you.
Their tastes may not be the same.
—George Bernard Shaw

You know the Golden Rule, of course. Virtually every religion and culture incorporates this basic moral code that we should treat other people the way we would like to be treated. In the Christian faith, it reads, "Thou shalt love thy neighbor as thyself." In the Jewish faith, "That which is hateful to you, do not do to your fellow." In the Buddhist teachings, "Hurt not others in ways that you yourself would find hurtful." In Islam, "Wish for your brother, what you wish for yourself." Confucius said, "Never impose on others what you would not choose for yourself."

Empathy, however, is something altogether *different*. Empathy is *not* treating someone else as you would want to be treated; rather, it is understanding how someone else would *want* to be treated. It's not about you.

Think of it like this. Perhaps your passion is fine wines. You enjoy wine with meals. You collect rare vintages. When dining out with friends, everyone looks to you. You're the one who reviews the wine menu and consults with the sommelier. You've invested in a personal wine cellar. Your dream vacation is a trip to Napa or Bordeaux.

For your birthday, you requested a subscription to *Wine Enthusiast*—and with good reason, as fine wines are your passion. So when the holidays come around, would it be appropriate to buy *Wine Enthusiast* subscriptions for everyone on your team? It would not.

You see the difference, right? Should a leader treat people well and with kindness and compassion? Of course. Should a leader treat people *exactly* as he or she would want to be treated? Of course not. Not everyone wants to be treated the way you want to be treated. *As a leader, it is your job to figure out how other people—other individuals—want to be treated.*

I work with a company that wanted to reward a particularly outstanding employee, Virginia, and with good reason. Virginia had outperformed every other teammate on a very lucrative project. It was, to put it mildly, a pretty big deal. Since the entire company was going to benefit from Virginia's efforts, it was decided that the entire company, including the heads of other departments, would be part of a huge congratulatory party recognizing Virginia's hard work.

Great idea, right?

Not really. In fact, it was a terrible idea. While Virginia's managers realized that she is hardworking and smart, they failed to take into account that she is also shy and reserved. Virginia didn't feel honored by the party. She felt mortified. As she said to me (privately, of course), "I just did my job. I wish they would just leave me alone. I hate this attention."

My college-aged daughter found the following question on a psychology test: "Nancy's parents gave her a slice of apple pie when she made good grades. Is this an example of positive reinforcement, negative reinforcement, or 'we don't have enough information'?"

My daughter responded the same way nearly every student in the class did—the apple pie was positive reinforcement. When she got her test back, though, my daughter was distraught to see that the professor had marked her response as incorrect.

To be truthful, I was initially surprised as well. What was this professor thinking? But then it came to me: *I like apple pie ... but what if Nancy doesn't?* What if she's allergic to apple pie? What if it is her sister's favored dessert but not hers? Do we have a real understanding of Nancy's parents' motives? Do we have enough information to understand Nancy herself?

You see, apple pie might be your favorite dessert. For you, it might be nectar of the gods. If pressed, you might request apple pie for your last meal. To put it into twenty-first-century terms, however, "It's *not* all about you."

Measuring your empathy

So maybe part of our formal education should be training in empathy.
Imagine how different the world would be if, in fact,
that were "reading, writing, arithmetic, empathy."
—Neil deGrasse Tyson

I work with a charismatic executive, Daniel, who has made the shift from energetic entrepreneur to chief operating officer of a fast-growing North American B2B marketing company. Daniel is charming, self-deprecating, gregarious, and energetic—a real people person—but an initial assessment also revealed that Daniel had *zero* empathy.

When Daniel and I considered the circumstances of our initial meeting, neither of us was surprised by the assessment findings. That first appointment had been at a local coffee shop. I arrived and spotted him right away as he reclined, talking loudly on his cell phone, oblivious to the people around him. I repeatedly tried to catch his eye, but he disregarded me. Even though he had requested the meeting, he practically ignored me. When he finally got off the phone, he scarcely greeted me before plunging into the topic at hand.

Driven? Yes. Empathetic? Decidedly not. Daniel was not accustomed to understanding or considering others' thoughts or feelings. Empathy had not been a behavior essential to his success as a serial entrepreneur. Now, however, that he was leading a company—and a company of some size—Daniel's lack of empathy was noticeable. Despite his gifts for business development and innovation, he simply couldn't predict how individuals would respond to his actions. He routinely misjudged the impact of his words, which resulted in lost efficiency and productivity.

To his credit, though, Daniel was—and is—*humble* (another essential leadership trait), and he was willing to develop the empathy to be a successful leader and run a successful company. He was also extremely likeable.

The transformation, of course, would take time, so one of the things I suggested was that Daniel surround himself with empathetic people and let them guide him, which is *not* a suggestion many leaders are willing to consider. But again, Daniel's humility allowed him to start running his ideas—particularly any changes he wanted to make to the company—by other people before announcing them to his staff. He also began taking the extra step of running e-mails by someone else before clicking the Send button.

Do you have insufficient empathy? Or perhaps too much? It can happen. If you have a track record of hiring the wrong people, if you seem to alienate colleagues or friends unwittingly, or if you are surprised by feedback from your board of directors, you do not have sufficient empathy. You are not able to understand what others are thinking or predict their behavior. Now that empathy has come up, plug it into your self-awareness battery. If you know empathy is important and you take a good look around and begin to wonder whether you are empathetic enough, you're on your way to meeting the empathy challenge.

I work with a client, Sam, known for his huge, caring heart. He cares not just about individuals but also about his community and humanity in general. His intense interest, however, can be off-putting at the individual level. Coworkers found his steady, unblinking gaze to be overwhelming. He had the habit of leaning forward and "into" people, giving the impression that he was staring them down. Some questioned, jokingly, whether Sam was trying to read their minds.

Sam was no Houdini, of course, but in his effort to give coworkers his undivided attention, Sam ended up becoming his own distraction. He had to be coached into reining in his empathetic behavior and showing it in deliberate, measured doses. Unlike leaders with low empathy, Sam had to learn to break eye contact periodically. He also had to hold himself back, to allow others the room to speak more.

So where do you, as a leader, stand on the empathy spectrum? Sometimes, just honestly answering the question, "Do I have the ability to understand the feelings of someone who works for me?" can help you self-identify. You can also ask others (whom you trust to be honest), work with a leadership coach (who will hopefully be honest), or self-administer an online assessment.

Bear in mind too that empathy is required on many fronts. A leader with great empathy for individuals may struggle to understand groups. Researchers find, time and time again, that there is not an automatic transference of empathy or the ability to understand others. It is easier to develop empathy for people whom we see as kindred spirits—whether they are of similar race, culture, education, background, field, class, or management level. The greatest challenge then is to develop empathy for those who are not like us—not just for people from different backgrounds and cultures but also for individuals and departments within the organization who serve functions and roles very different from our own.

Increasing your empathy

> I think we all have empathy.
> We may not have enough courage to display it.
> —Maya Angelou

I recently heard a funny story from my neighbor, Louise. "On the way into work this morning, I got a phone call from one of our company's senior executives," she said. "I was immediately anxious to see his name on my phone because I never hear from him directly. I was even more nervous as he hemmed and hawed in the beginning of the call, saying he'd wanted to meet with me the day before but couldn't track me down. My hands started sweating as he said he hated to do this kind of thing by phone but didn't have any choice. My heart was racing by the time he said that he had hired somebody new, and I became somewhat dizzy when he finally said that a new employee was starting in our office that day."

By this point in the story, I was concerned too. "What happened?" I asked.

Louise paused for effect and shrugged. "He wanted to know if I would mind moving to another desk, so the new person, who is fresh out of school, could sit closer to his team."

Louise breathed a huge sigh of relief and then laughed. "Heck of a way to start the day, don't you think?"

The senior executive in this story didn't entirely lack empathy. Indeed, he showed great empathy for the new employee. What he needed to work on, though, was developing empathetic behavior to the point that it is automatic—a reflex, if you will. He should have predicted Louise's thoughts and response to his setting the stage for what he wanted to communicate. The buildup was not necessary and, in fact, somewhat cruel.

I'm currently coaching another wonderful leader, Margaret, who routinely earns rave reviews from colleagues, coworkers, and employees. What's her trick?

"It's not all that hard," she says. "I take time to figure out each person when I meet with him or her. In the beginning, it would take me a while, but now, when I focus, it takes about ten minutes."

Plenty of leaders would balk at the idea of spending ten minutes to meet with a colleague. Still, by doing ten minutes of prep work, checking a person's LinkedIn profile, doing an online search, and asking other people, a leader can save a lot of getting-to-know-you time, as well as less damage-control time. The research also increases understanding, of course, which is one major way you can increase your empathy. With understanding comes your ability to empathize and reasonably predict reactions from teammates and followers. As I've said, you don't have to like all your employees; you just have to understand them.

A leader must think before speaking. A leader has to be quiet. And in that mental pause, a leader has to consider his or her intent, his or her motive, and then consider how the other person will receive the information.

Great leaders work at developing empathetic behavior. I had the pleasure of working with a high-ranking financial executive in New York City, Nick, who has the misfortune of working in an admittedly ruthless workplace environment. Year after year, though, Nick not only emerges unscathed but highly regarded.

"You continue to have a great reputation. How does that happen?" I asked.

"I have to work at it, of course," he responded, "but I also read a lot. Ever since I was a kid, I liked reading about historical figures and great leaders, and I still do. I think it shapes who I am now."

Nick's leadership instincts are backed up by research. A recent study from *The Guardian* confirms that the simple act of reading literary fiction improves empathy. Additionally, researchers have found that literary fiction authored by writers such as Charles Dickens sharpens our ability to understand others' emotions more than thrillers or romance novels.

Another simple way to increase empathy is by *listening*. Indeed, there is a strong corollary between people with low empathy and people who are poor listeners.

Not everyone is quick to embrace empathetic behavior as a leadership tool. Richard, the fast-tracked executive I told you about at the beginning of this chapter, was a tough case. I had to work long and hard to get him to come around and understand the upside of empathy. Since he was wildly successful in practically every other area of leadership, I had to be pretty blunt.

"You know what?" I said. "You're just going to have to *pretend* to be interested in the people you work with. Ask about their weekends. Listen to their stories. Ask follow-up questions."

I pressed on with my assignment. "In fact, the *less* you know someone, the *more* interest you need to show. Don't go for the people who are just like you. Start with people you are not comfortable with. Learn their family members' names. Write them down if you have to. I honestly don't care if you have to fake it for a while. *Just do it.*"

Lo and behold, some months later, Richard's empathy scores were considerably higher. And behaving more empathetically came more naturally to him. In fact, he said it began happening automatically.

An even greater success story to me, though, was when Richard said, "All of this makes sense to me now, but you know what? I was wrong. These people—my coworkers and my direct reports—are actually interesting. I'm glad I know and understand them better now. It makes it easier to work with them.

"I think I get it now."

Developing and increasing empathy requires time, focus, concentration, and commitment. Developing empathy is like a multistep, ongoing project.

So what behaviors can you develop to increase your level of empathy?

- Slow down.
- Survey your surroundings.
- Listen.
- Read body language.
- Check for understanding.
- Don't presume.
- Put yourself in someone else's shoes.
- Seek out the other side.

Slow down. When you are running from one meeting to another and from one project to another, you cannot be strategic and get into people's minds. Slow down. Take a breath. Think ahead. Give yourself a minute to prepare. A busy father I know once ended up in couples therapy because he had a hard time making the transition from work to home. The therapist made a simple suggestion: "When you pull into the driveway, turn off the car, turn off the radio, and then start turning off work. Take a minute to think about your family and what you want to say and do with them *before* you get out of the car and walk into the house."

In other words, *slow down. Think.* As you rush to your office or to another meeting, slow down, look people in the eye, and concentrate on them. With practice, you'll find it possible to do this in a few seconds.

Survey your surroundings. Empathetic leaders are conscious of their surroundings. Look around and *see* what and who is around you. I met with a CEO of a retail company who once told me he had what he called a "Doppler." He had mastered the art of surveying a room so well that the minute he walked in, he could sense the mood and could see where groups of people were congregating. Within seconds, he knew exactly where he had to go, what he had to do, and with whom he had to speak.

Listen. All too often, when one person is speaking during a conversation, the other person is thinking—thinking about what he or she is going to say next. Stop. Listen. Listen with your ears, and listen with your eyes. Leaders with high empathy stop everything else and listen carefully until the other person stops speaking. Even on a phone call, they do not multitask but listen intently. In this manner, they are able to catch what is *not* said as well as what is being said. By listening, these leaders pick up on nuances—the stuff people really mean but never tell you. The best leaders can figure out what others are thinking because they can skillfully read between the lines.

Read body language. Much of communication is unspoken. Try to match facial expressions to the words. Notice the regional differences in the way people communicate. My husband, who is from the Midwest, had to learn this the hard way. When he first moved to the South, hospitable neighbors told him, "You should come over sometime," which he took for an invitation. Imagine their surprise when he showed up on their front porches unannounced, because, in fact, they meant, "Perhaps we will see you sometime."

Check for understanding. After you have listened, make a habit of saying, "Okay. Let me make sure I understand." For example, after a meeting, ask for the thoughts of someone else who attended. Gauge your assessment based on theirs. Actually ask for other people's insights: "Did I read this person right?" Was your interpretation in line with others'? Validate, confirm, corroborate. Be deliberate—until you are confident that you are reading situations accurately.

Don't presume. My mother, like so many others, urged me not to judge others based on their appearance. "Get to know them," she'd say. "You never know what someone else may be going through." A dear friend made this same point to me in a revealing story. She'd gone to a fine restaurant one evening and waited at the hostess station behind an unusual couple. The young man was handsome and looked as if he belonged at the restaurant, but his companion was wearing a long fur coat and a ridiculous-looking hat and draped herself across the young man in a way my friend felt was entirely inappropriate. Later, during dinner, the out-of-place woman approached my friend's table. My friend recognized her and realized, to her chagrin, that the woman was wearing the coat because she was cold, that the woman's companion was her young son, and that the woman was wearing the hat to cover her bald head—the result of chemotherapy. The woman my friend judged was not only an acquaintance but also a cancer patient.

Even a highly trained, Ivy League–educated, circuit court judge has to wait until hearing all the facts before rendering a decision. Until you have all the facts, withhold judgment. Don't presume.

Put yourself in someone else's shoes. I mentioned earlier that, as a management trainee, I was required to fill different positions at the utility company where I worked. You can literally put yourself into someone else's role. Consider working on the manufacturing floor of your company or spending a day riding with a sales rep. Immerse yourself in the culture, in the job, in the situation.

Seek out the other side. Finally, remember that there is always another side, and as a leader, you must be more than just aware of the fact; you have to seek it out. I once worked with a loud colleague who seemed to get even louder—and borderline obnoxious—when we were out to lunch, particularly when we were out to lunch with clients. Since I am a fairly quiet person, it was annoying and at times downright maddening. Then one day, my colleague shared that he was losing his hearing. To this day, I wish that instead of presuming, I had slowed down enough to ask myself whether it was possible that something else was going on. If I had, perhaps I wouldn't have been so annoyed. Perhaps I would have been understanding.

Leadership roundup

As the third component of a behavior-based approach to leadership, empathy is a natural follow-up to self-control. Those who are self-aware enough to know that self-control is important will likewise be able to see the wisdom of employing an empathetic style in the corporate arena. As the saying goes, "You catch more flies with honey than you do with vinegar." Empathy is often overlooked among busy executives. The notion that empathetic behavior would actually make a difference in employee morale, productivity, efficiency, and profitability simply doesn't cross their minds. But empathy does matter. Without it, you'll find yourself fighting a losing battle as a leader.

- Empathy isn't about caring in the traditional sense. When you're compassionate or sympathetic, you are emotionally committed. You actually do care. When you're empathetic, you're on a distinctly non-emotional plane. You understand what the person is feeling and why, and you understand how that person might react under any set of circumstances, be they positive or negative. But you're not emotional. That's an important thing to remember.
- You don't have to like your employees to be empathetic toward them.
- Not everyone will think or react as you do. Thus, self-awareness comes into play. You have to know yourself and avoid projecting

how you would feel on others as you seek to understand followers through the empathetic process.

- Empathy can be measured. If you are finding strife, turnover, intimidation, fear, and other negativity in the company, upper management is likely missing at least some measure of empathy.
- Empathy can be increased. As a self-aware leader, you can make a conscious choice to increase your empathy for your followers. Taking the time to understand your followers will enhance your ability to be empathetic toward them. This, in turn, will build. Soon your empathetic behavior will become second nature.

Chapter 5

Humility

Do you wish to rise? Begin by descending.
You plan a tower that will pierce the clouds?
Lay first the foundation of humility.
—Saint Augustine

Cade Pope, a twelve-year-old boy, set out on a quest to determine which professional football team he should support. His home state of Oklahoma does not have its own pro team, so it's easy to imagine Cade trying to determine which team was "his" every NFL Sunday. Which colors should he wear? Which player stats should he Google?

The questions, which were very real to him, are likely insignificant (and unfathomable) to some adults. The point remains, though: Cade wanted a team. He wanted to be a fan, so he took the unusual step of handwriting letters to the owners of all thirty-two NFL teams, explaining his dilemma and asking each owner to help him decide.

Out of thirty-two NFL owners, one actually personally responded to Cade. Only one. And just like Cade, Jerry Richardson, the owner of the Carolina Panthers—valued at more than a billion dollars—handwrote his response, which read, in part, "We would be honored if our Carolina Panthers became your team. We would make you proud by the classy way we would represent you."

That is humility in action. In his charming response, NFL owner Jerry Richardson was both modest and respectful. And mind you, he was writing to a child—a child to whom no other NFL owner responded.

Like the other powerful, influential, busy NFL owners, Richardson had options. Plenty of them. He could have tossed Cade's letter in the trash. He could have had a staff member respond to Cade. He could have sent a form letter. He could have sent a team trinket (indeed, he did include a Panthers helmet with his handwritten response, signed by defensive leader Luke Kuechly). Cade probably would have been thrilled with any type of response. But Richardson handwrote his note. He gave a total stranger—a stranger without power or influence or fame or fortune—a warm and personal response.

Humility is a measure of character that differentiates great leaders from the rest. It's the recognition and acknowledgment that a person is codependent on the world and on other people. It is understanding that no one can stand alone, whether in a community or in a business context. It is understanding that it's not all about you. Simply put, it is understanding that you cannot succeed alone.

Very arrogant people tend to be super independent and want to go it alone and take the credit. You probably know an arrogant leader. The one who throws others under the bus. The one who blames others—coworkers, employees, departments, or entire organizations—for failures and near misses. The one who knows it all and wants everyone to know it. The one who always speaks in first person singular, talking about "my" team and "my" people and "my" research. The one who constantly interrupts in an effort to show his or her knowledge and superiority.

Arrogant leaders may seem completely confident. However, when you scratch beneath the surface, you'll find that they are insecure and have all types of inferiority complexes and dysfunctional personalities. Well-rounded leaders are able to hold space for others, acknowledge they need other people, and are codependent on society and the world. They acknowledge that they are part of a bigger system—part of humanity.

Humility is the opposite of arrogance. It is the quality of being modest and respectful. A humble person both recognizes when he or she doesn't know all the answers *and* acknowledges that fact. In this way, a humble person is supremely self-confident and secure, overcoming insecurities to acknowledge shortcomings.

To be honest, I don't actually know which NFL team twelve-year-old Cade now claims as his own. I, however, am now a fan of Jerry Richardson.

Importance of humility

> Humility is not thinking less of yourself,
> it's thinking of yourself less.
> —C. S. Lewis

A common television sitcom plotline involves the lead character's inability or unwillingness to say "I love you." Inevitably, the character will stutter or feign laryngitis or resort to comic diversionary tactics—anything to avoid choking on those three little words. "I love you."

Sadly, there's a real-life parallel in the business world. An executive faced with an unfamiliar situation and fearful about appearing weak, vulnerable, or uninformed may stumble or become defensive—anything to avoid uttering the three little words *"I don't know."* Yet those three words mean much and on many levels. First, saying you don't know as a leader conveys humility to your followers. Second, your followers will jump to it in an effort to fill you in. When knowledge gaps get plugged, everybody wins. This is just one example of why humility matters and is the fourth component of a behavior-based approach to sound executive leadership.

David Dotlich and Peter Cairo, authors of *Why CEOs Fail*, state that arrogance is when "you're right, and everybody else is wrong." But when you've been paid and rewarded for "being right" for so very many years—as most leaders have—humility doesn't always come easily. In fact, humility can easily be construed as a liability. After all, no leader wants to look weak in front of his or her followers.

Arrogance, to a certain extent, seems inevitable when you get up to a high level of management. But there's no denying the ineffectiveness of such behavior. As Dotlich and Cairo point out, "Arrogance, from an organizational leadership perspective, is a kind of blinding belief in your own opinions. Under normal circumstances, smart leaders can see when they're being too stubborn, single-minded, and self-righteous. Unfortunately, most leaders today operate under highly stressful circumstances where they don't see how their actions are hurting themselves and their companies."

Being humble requires that leaders acknowledge their own shortcomings and recognize that they don't have all the answers. It requires being vulnerable. It requires bearing in mind that old adage, "You're only as good as your people." In short, it all blends together with the other core concepts of a behavior-based approach—self-awareness, self-control, and empathy. Based on my many years working as an executive coach, I can tell you that embracing these behavior-based leadership concepts is easier said than done. Humility is particularly problematic. Yet, time and time again, examples show that the most-effective leaders— those who inspire followership—score high on a humility scale. They surround themselves with good people, realizing that they don't know everything and recognizing what others can contribute. Humble leaders can thrive and see great success, drawing on the strengths and abilities of their teams and subject matter experts, without feeling threatened.

Arrogance, however, can creep up on you as a leader. If it does, your capacity to learn, to be creative, to be innovative, and to effectively lead will be diminished.

I once worked with a brilliant client, Celeste, who achieved executive-level status relatively early in her career, and with good reason: Celeste was intelligent, likeable, a good listener, and a fair arbiter. She had a lengthy history of working with her team to arrive at the "right" decision. This led to accolades piled upon accolades, which made Celeste feel it was appropriate to begin relying solely on her own sound judgment. After all, hadn't her judgment and decision-making been roundly admired and praised? So bit by bit, she stopped listening to the guidance and opinions of others. She began working in isolation. She became self-righteous. Some might have described her as arrogant. Predictably, Celeste began alienating the people around her. Eventually, she made a few critical mistakes, with only herself to blame.

The best leaders nurture humility, keeping it at the very core of their leadership style. For Celeste, the solution was simple: she had to return to her humble roots. From previous behavior, she knew what humble behavior required, and she had to once again make that behavior a priority. Celeste paused and took time to reevaluate her behavior. Recognizing that she had stopped asking for advice, she made a deliberate effort to begin—once again—calling on the counsel of the smart people around her. She asked questions, listened wholeheartedly, and considered other people's input before making decisions. Fortunately, Celeste's self-confidence in her decision-making abilities was not disrupted. She simply added other people's wisdom to hers. The result was exponential excellence.

We all fear being seen as weak or not knowing all the answers. But again, if we are humble and self-confident, we're okay with not knowing all the answers. When in doubt, remember, *you are not always right, and other people are not always wrong.*

Hyperactive humility

> Humility is like underwear;
> essential, but indecent if it shows.
> —Helen Nielson

It is possible, of course, to take humility to extremes, which is equally as ineffective as being arrogant. It you're too humble, you may be perceived as weak. So where's the balance?

When I consider the notion of a humility quotient, I see two extremes: arrogance on one end of the continuum and subservience on the other. Arrogance is perhaps the more common extreme in the working world. However, subservience can be just as problematic. A leader who is subservient has no backbone, as they say. A subservient leader is often treated as a doormat—a direct result of failing to have or show self-confidence. Remember, humility requires self-confidence.

True humility falls in the middle of the spectrum. Many humble people who aren't great leaders lack awareness of the importance of accountability and self-discipline and the necessity of achieving results. You can be humble while still holding yourself and others accountable. You can be assertive while still depending on other people. It's a collaborative approach. Those who get into trouble are the ones who are subservient, who do whatever others ask them to do. That's not humility. That's people-pleasing, which is not a healthy behavior. In addition, a person who is genuinely too humble can find it difficult to accomplish things. Coworkers can find it frustrating to work with leaders who are not decisive and authoritative when needed.

A strong leader can modulate his or her behavior, dialing it up or down as a situation requires. For example, in a crisis, a leader might need to dial down the humble behavior, to be viewed as strong and assuring. In other situations, a leader might need to dial up the humility, to ensure that others have a chance to be heard.

What we're talking about here are perceived *behaviors*. Arrogance is a perceived behavior, and subservience is a perceived behavior. Behaviors can be changed. As a coach, I don't advocate changing a *person*. Trying to change a person can be arduous, exhausting, and, ultimately, unproductive. Changing a *behavior* is more easily accomplished and more productive, effective, and worthwhile.

Let's consider an anecdote to illustrate why humility is important and why a balance between too much and too little is highly desirable. Like so many other students, when my daughter Michelle was in elementary school, she read *Flat Stanley*, Jeff Brown's charming story about a child who is literally flattened. While there are, of course, downsides to being two-dimensional, Flat Stanley finds a few benefits, realizing that he can slide under doors, fly like a kite, and fit into an envelope for mailing. Part of my daughter's school assignment involved mailing a paper Flat Stanley to various places and people and then reporting on Stanley's adventures.

Of her own choosing, Michelle sent her Flat Stanley to our hometown mayor, Pat McCrory. I was somewhat hesitant, wondering how a very busy politician would react—if at all—to a child, a constituent who couldn't even vote. I understood, even if Michelle didn't, the pressing responsibilities and pressures and constant tugs our Charlotte mayor faced. Imagine Michelle's delight, then—and mine—when she received, in return mail, a photo of Flat Stanley seated at the mayor's desk!

Mayor McCrory (who later became governor of North Carolina) surely had no ulterior motives. It would not surprise me, though, to learn that his behavior—humility—is a factor in his political success. As a group, politicians often excel at behaving humbly in front of their constituents, understanding better than other leaders that being approachable—part of humble behavior—can help garner votes.

Again, successful leadership all comes back to followership. In many ways, humble leaders can attract and influence followers (e.g., voters) by displaying basic courtesy and, even more simply, putting to use the good manners drilled into us as young children.

Think about it. Where an impolite person may come across as arrogant, rude, entitled, and superior, effectively *repelling* followers, a polite person comes across as approachable, kind, thoughtful, and caring, effectively *attracting* followers.

As much as anything, humility involves good manners. Politicians can be polite. Multimillionaires can be polite. Celebrities can be polite. Busy executives can be polite. And so can you. Humility is a behavior, and behavior is a matter of *choice*.

Your humility quotient

> Pride is concerned with *who* is right.
> Humility is concerned with *what* is right.
> —Ezra T. Benson

When I do my 360-degree interviews, I try to assess the leader's *humility quotient*, asking coworkers where they would place the leader on a continuum from arrogance to humility to subservience. I'm looking for someone who doesn't fall at either extreme. The best leaders are able to act a little more or a little less humble, as the situation requires.

Leaders who fall into that midrange of the humility continuum are often extraordinarily gifted leaders who acknowledge when they don't know something or don't have all the answers. They feel secure because they are actually supremely smart. You might argue that a gifted leader can afford to be humble, but I'd argue that being humble is what led him or her to that knowledge.

To change your own humility quotient, you'll first need to determine where you fall in the spectrum. This, in itself, requires humility. Humility is not a matter of what you think of yourself but more a matter of what others think of you. It's not a reflection; it's a perception.

In determining your own humility quotient, I recommend that you seek the perceptions of two groups:

- coworkers (including peers, superiors, direct reports, vendors, and clients) known to be honest and direct
- your personal advisory board—trusted individuals outside of work, including friends, family members, and mentors

These are the people you can ask, "Where do you think I stand on the continuum of subservience to arrogance? In other words, do I show humility? Can you think of specific examples where I have shown humility? Can you think of specific examples where I could have shown more (or less) humility? What behaviors am I exhibiting that make you say this?"

If you make it clear that you're seeking honest perspectives and examples, these individuals can provide invaluable—and *accurate*—advice that can help you determine the extent to which you may want to change your behavior.

Ordinary humble behavior requires the most extraordinary—and simplest—of efforts. As I mentioned in a previous chapter, my first real job was as a trainee in one of the largest companies in town. One day, during my lunch break, as I was rushing down the street to get back to the office, I thought I heard someone call my name. Knowing I risked being late—and believing myself to be a nobody in such a big business town—I stepped up my pace, only to hear my name again, clearly called out. I had no choice: I spun around to see who was calling me. And to this day, I'm relieved I did. It was one of the senior executives in the company, someone I would have sworn didn't even know my name. He was merely greeting me, making sure to acknowledge me, a "lowly" trainee. In an instant, I went from feeling like one of the masses to someone worth knowing. That manager didn't have to greet me. He didn't have to go out of his way. We weren't in an elevator; we were on the sidewalk of a busy downtown street during lunchtime. Still, he did. With one simple action, he displayed humility. He made me feel important. And deliberately or not, he established himself as a leader worth following.

Showing humility requires time and effort—perhaps more so than other behaviors described in this book. However, the considerable short-term effort will surely pay off long term. Your ability to influence determines your ability to lead. Why wouldn't you be humble? Why wouldn't you act humbly? You're not relinquishing stature. You're not abandoning prestige. In humble behavior, you increase your followership, which is essential to leadership.

So you've measured your humility quotient, and now you want to find ways to best balance your humility when it comes to dealing with your followers. Here's another bowl of alphabet soup for you: CALM—communicate, ask, listen, and make time. Just like the ART and WAIT bowls you encountered earlier, you should apply CALM as you go through each day at work. Let's take a closer look!

Communicate. Venture out of your office, away from your computer; put down your smartphone; and *talk.* Make a practice of talking to people at every level in your organization—the cashier, the CFO, the human resources officer, the janitor. Answer questions, return calls, and respond to e-mails in a timely manner. Communication is a big part of humility in leadership and will help you create a legacy.

Ask. Don't be afraid to ask questions. Humble leaders ask lots of questions and are open to feedback, understanding that inquisitiveness is essential to humility. Openness and curiosity make a person a good student of his or her feelings as well as the world around him or her. Humble leaders are also able to ask for help, understanding that by doing so they aren't only helping themselves but also helping the helpers. In admitting you need help, you're creating a wonderful opportunity for someone to help you. Asking someone else for assistance can be the highest form of flattery and a compliment to others.

Listen. Even more important than talking is listening, whether you're seeking out someone else's perspective or not. Be open and approachable. Allow people to disagree with you. Humble people make eye contact and give body language that they are approachable and willing to give their time. Aggressive, competitive leaders will walk down the hall oblivious to the fact that people are around them. Humble people give that extra thirty seconds. They pause. They listen.

Make time. Never think so much of yourself that you think you don't have time for others. Give yourself an extra thirty seconds to walk to a meeting so that you can greet coworkers in the hall. Make time to respond to e-mails—even if only to say, "I got it, thanks." Return phone calls. Make eye contact.

I recently met with John, a senior marketing executive in a global company. John is an exceptional leader and one of those delightful clients from whom I learn a great deal. Since he already exhibits so many of the great attributes and behaviors of effective leaders, I was eager to hear his take on humility. In John's words, "People are not about efficiency. Humble leaders make time for others. They give individuals undivided attention." You might think you don't have time for this; you might think you are too busy running from one thing to another. But people are not about efficiency. Working with people is not a place for a leader to cut corners. People are about being recognized and looked in the eye and spoken to.

A few days later, in the midst of an exceptionally busy workday, I took my dog for a quick walk, knowing I'd get back to the office just in time for my next conference call. About fifteen yards ahead of me, I spotted a talkative neighbor. As I quickly assessed my options, I considered cutting the walk short and turning around to avoid him. I also considered stepping up my pace, indicating that I didn't have time to chat. However, my client's lesson on humility was still ringing in my ears. I decided to forget efficiency, make time, and be warm and approachable.

As it turned out, my talkative neighbor didn't have time for me! As I neared, he was the one who turned and dashed into the house, mumbling something about having an appointment.

My lesson in humility was suddenly tossed on its ear. Who was I to think that I was the only busy one?

And speaking of busy, let's take a moment to look at telephone versus e-mail communication. I'll talk more about communication later, but it does figure into our discussion about humility, so I might as well tackle some of the issues right here. Modern technology is a wonderful thing, indeed. Thanks to smartphones, Wi-Fi, social media, apps, and laptops, we can constantly be in touch with people. And just as it's important not to be controlled and distracted by the onslaught of communications, it's also important to *respond*. Not every e-mail requires a response, of course, but many do. As a leader, you surely can discern the difference between an employee seeking your feedback and a mass mailing requiring no response. If you don't respond to the employee, it's an insult. It's as if, during the course of a meeting, you turn your face away when a colleague speaks to you.

Answer your e-mail. Even if it's a simple "Thanks, I got it" or "Let me get back to you." I recently sent a long, well-considered proposal to a prospect. I knew it would take quite a while to digest; however, I was impressed to get an immediate response: "I wanted to let you know I received the proposal and will get back to you in a few days."

In fact, while we're on the topic, why not just pick up the phone and call the person who sent you an e-mail? Or better still, walk over to his or her desk? These are the acts of a humble leader.

Good karma

Humility has other advantages. One of them is it fosters good karma. Whether you believe in karma or not, I'm sure most of us believe that there is some kind of universal justice in the world, however random it might be. What goes around comes around. If you behave poorly and with arrogance, it can come back to bite you hard. On the other hand, if you behave well and with humility, you'll build good karma that might help you someday.

Some years back, I worked with Carrie, a sales executive. She was a star at putting on her best face and putting forth her best efforts, even with one particularly difficult client, a company whose employees treated Carrie dismissively. They viewed Carrie as a vendor and wanted to make sure she was well aware of her second-class status. They would keep her waiting for meetings. They would not return phone calls. Oftentimes, they were rude, interrupting Carrie or blaming her for situations she hadn't caused.

Carrie didn't complain. And she didn't behave like a doormat. She simply behaved as a professional. A few years passed, and before too long, Carrie quit her job and took a management position at the same company where she'd been treated badly. And yes, you guessed it: Carrie ended up managing the very individuals who had treated her so poorly.

Fortunately for them, Carrie isn't the vindictive sort. But think how much better things would be for *everyone* if those individuals had chosen to treat Carrie the vendor the way they would have treated (and ended up treating) Carrie the manager.

Leadership roundup

Humility can be elusive in the executive suite. Leaders are typically type A personalities who have driven hard and long to climb the ladder to the top. They've been right more times than not about critical business decisions and moves, and they've acquired enough knowledge of their industry to make them formidable in even casual exchanges. Thus, humility is often overlooked.

Yet, as the fourth component of a behavior-based approach to executive leadership, humility should not be forgotten or overlooked. It goes hand in hand with empathy. If you can't be humble enough to know that you don't know everything and aren't always right, how can you be empathetic enough to understand how your followers will think, feel, and act if they get into a situation where they're up against the gun and are unsure of how to deliver what is expected? Without self-awareness and self-control, empathy and humility will surely be lacking.

- You might say that humility is the opposite of arrogance. As such, the humble way is the better way when it comes to leadership. Arrogance brings with it the probability of negative feedback, diminished employee morale, higher turnover, lowered efficiency, unclear communication, fear, and reduced profitability. Humility will net you the opposite results because it encourages a happier work environment for everyone.
- Too much humility can make you look weak and ineffectual as a leader. A lack of tactful assertion when the chips are down can be just as damaging to a company as an arrogant leader. As with all aspects of behavioral leadership, you must find a harmonious balance between all the components.
- Increase your humility quotient through the CALM method. Communicate, ask questions, listen, and make time.

Chapter 6

Integrity

The supreme quality for leadership is unquestionably integrity.
Without it, no real success is possible, no matter whether it is
on a section gang, a football field, in an army, or in an office.
—Dwight D. Eisenhower

I once worked with Taylor, the head of a very large agency in the
southeastern United States. As the agency's chief executive, Taylor
was accountable to countless public and private constituents as well as
crowds of colleagues and coworkers and, let's not forget, the media. The
scrutiny was crushing. Every business decision Taylor made was made in
the spotlight, not only publicized but also judged. How can any leader
perform—much less succeed—under such circumstances? The answer
is simple: with integrity.

More than just a sound business practice (which it is), integrity is
profoundly essential to successful leadership. A leader with high
integrity inspires followership, and in successful organizations,
integrity is modeled from the top. As with the previous components of
a behavior-based approach to leadership, integrity is but one piece of
a fully integrated puzzle. Self-awareness leads to a natural progression
from one component to the next. Taken together the various aspects of
behavioral leadership constitute a powerful and unique way to manage
a business.

Professor Thomas Dunfee of the Wharton School says, "Personal integrity is as important as executive skill in business dealings ... Setting an example from the top has a ripple effect ... After nearly three decades in business, 10 years as chief executive of a Big Eight accounting firm, I have learned that the standards set at the top filter throughout a company."

Russell E. Palmer of the Palmer Group (and former dean of the Wharton School) says, "A company that fails to take steps to produce a climate conducive to positive work-related ethical attitudes may create a vacuum in which employees so predisposed may foster a frontier-style, everyone for themselves mentality."

Followers realize that leaders with integrity will make decisions for everyone's good. Remember the question I always ask during my 360-degree interviews on behalf of my coaching clients: *Would you follow this person over a hill, not knowing what's on the other side?* Very often, if I get a negative response to this question, it is because of lack of integrity or *perceived* lack of integrity, which is equally as damaging.

Leaders with strong and recognizable integrity inspire followership. Workers can, and will, follow these leaders "over the hill," trusting that all will be well.

Now, I admit, I am fortunate that the vast majority of my clients are perceived to have high integrity. Every once in a while, however, I run into a responder who does not trust the person I am coaching.

I can see how this happens. Of all the behaviors I coach, integrity may be the one least examined by leaders. I believe this is because we all think we behave with integrity. Did we not learn the difference between right and wrong when we were children? Of course we did. However, every one of us can readily point to business examples where a lapse of integrity, values, or ethics led to dire consequences.

- Arthur Andersen, once regarded as one of the finest and most reputable accounting firms in the world, was toppled by revelations that it looked the other way when one of its largest clients, Enron, engaged in questionable accounting practices. As you may recall, Enron took advantage of accounting loopholes and poor financial reporting to hide billions of dollars of debt and pressured Andersen to maintain the facade. In the end, both companies essentially keeled over, with executives on both sides sentenced to prison.

- Even twenty years later, Exxon's reputation has yet to recover from the unethical behavior leading to and following the devastating Valdez oil spill. It began simply, albeit it tragically, enough, with an oil tanker running aground and creating the second-largest oil spill in US history. But as the seamy undersides of previous business deals were exposed and as Exxon leaders failed to accept responsibility, make apologies, or work with the media (i.e., communicate), the oil company's reputation was devastated.

- Donations to the Livestrong cancer charity plummeted in 2013 when its founder and cancer survivor, Lance Armstrong, stepped down amid allegations of taking performance-enhancing drugs during his highly accolated cycling career. In 2009, Livestrong raised something like $41 million. In 2013, following Armstrong's shameful admission of guilt, donations were reported to be $15 million—a 34 percent drop from the previous tumultuous year.

From the Latin word *integer*, *integrity* means complete or whole, acting honestly and fairly with a steadfast adherence to a moral or ethical code. This code, however, is not always absolutely defined. While most of us would agree upon the basics—for example, do not kill, do not harm, and be kind—much of what constitutes integrity is very much subject to interpretation, not only fluctuating from culture to culture but also from individual to individual.

I once interviewed an employee, Lilliane, who complained about the lack of integrity of her company's owners. Lilliane voiced her opinion, loudly and frequently, to the point that the company owners were not only alarmed but also confused, so I probed for examples and tried to understand her definition of integrity. Given the chance to elaborate, Lilliane was adamant and clear: the company had a healthy profit margin, and she felt this should translate into the owners giving more to charity. On the surface, Lilliane had a point and certainly had good intentions; digging a little deeper, though, I realized that Lilliane— kindhearted as she was—did not have the business savvy to understand the cost of running the business. She did not give credit to the fact that the owners were using the high profit margins to reinvest in the company, give employees good bonuses, and minimize debt. In other words, although disgruntled, Lilliane was benefiting from the way the owners ran the business.

Still, Lilliane believed that her organization's owners were greedy, which compromised their integrity. Although I do believe that greed can compromise integrity, I did not share her interpretation that goals for strong profit margins indicated a lack of integrity. The owners agreed and were greatly relieved to understand that Lilliane's use of the word *integrity* really didn't apply to the situation at hand.

In his book *Cowboy Ethics: What Wall Street Can Learn from the Code of the West*, James P. Owen is very specific about ethical business behavior, laying out ten specific rules:

Code of the West

(1) Live each day with courage.
(2) Take pride in your work.
(3) Always finish what you start.
(4) Do what has to be done.
(5) Be tough, but fair.
(6) When you make a promise, keep it.

(7) Ride for the brand.
(8) Talk less and say more.
(9) Remember that some things aren't for sale.
(10) Know where to draw the line.

I rather like this code, particularly number six, "When you make a promise, keep it." However, I'm not saying that it's necessary for a leader to have a written code. It is, though, healthy and worthwhile to consider what ethical behaviors look like in a leader or in a business. In my 360-degree interviews, I routinely ask, "How would you rate this leader on integrity?" And I'm swift to follow up with "What is your definition of integrity?" Since leaders who seek executive coaching tend to have high integrity, I typically hear comments like the following:

- She always takes ownership of the issue, whether it's good or bad.
- He does whatever it takes to support our team. I trust him.
- He's honest and consistent. He does what he says he's going to do.
- She does a good job instilling trust and is respectful of our opinions.
- He's fair. He has strong values and morals. He treats everyone fairly.

I will always remember the employee who enthusiastically gave his employer an integrity score of 10 out of 10. Given such a high score, I probed, "Can you give me an example?" Without hesitation, the employee said, "Yes! He doesn't check his iPhone during meetings!"

Although his response made me smile, what he was describing is not integrity. Focusing on the meeting at hand, listening to people speaking, and not checking one's phone is a matter of simple civility. But this example points out the necessity of asking the people I interview, "How do *you* define integrity?" Integrity isn't courtesy; it's larger than that. Integrity requires courage. It requires moral strength. It requires steadfastness and consistency. It requires ethics—not just knowing the difference between right and wrong but *behaving* accordingly.

As a reminder, we are speaking here of integrity as regarded in Western culture and, more specifically, in a workplace. Even so, behaving with or without integrity at work will inevitably spill over into one's personal life. And vice versa. Can a person display high integrity in business while cheating on a spouse in his or her personal life? While I certainly have an opinion, I'll leave that to you to decide. I'm not here to judge values or morals. I'm here to point out the behaviors of highly successful leaders and to show you how—and to encourage you—to follow their examples.

The snowball effect

> So near is falsehood to truth that
> a wise man would do well
> not to trust himself on the narrow edge.
> —Cicero

In most societies, we assume that people have integrity. We assume that our Starbucks barista will give us the proper change; that the person wearing a uniform is, in fact, a member in good standing of the police force; that when our friends and colleagues speak to us, they are speaking the truth.

Yet, time and time again, we are presented with case studies of leaders who have behaved without integrity.

Why do leaders struggle with this fundamental behavior? After all, most of us learn from parents, teachers, and coaches at a very young age the difference between right and wrong. Do these leaders not have this basic understanding? Do they not have a personal code of ethics?

Of course they do. But there are other factors: the sheer stress of shouldering the burden of leadership and the fear of disappointing employees, partners, or shareholders. For the most part, the executives I coach are good, well-intentioned leaders. If their integrity is in question—if people believe they behave unethically—it likely began with an insignificant misstep that mushroomed into something much greater. An incalculable toe over the line, impossible to retract. This was exactly the situation one of my clients faced. My client, the CEO, was appalled to learn that his controller had been "creative" with the corporate bookkeeping. The CEO was heartbroken, as the controller had been a longtime employee of the company, an upstanding citizen, and a well-intentioned executive. The incalculable toe over the line, however, cost him his job. The CEO could not afford even the smallest hint of impropriety as he reported results to shareholders.

Sometimes, a loss of integrity is related to moral licensing (referred to in chapter 3, "Self-Control"), where individuals give themselves "permission" to act without integrity. For example, a manager may say to herself, "It's okay to fudge the spreadsheet because I am saving people's jobs." Or an executive may convince himself, "I am actually very good at doing this one thing, so pretending to be good at this other thing is okay." Or a leader may say, "I serve my church, my community, and the local schools. It's okay to cheat on my expense report." In a previous chapter, I spoke about discipline and moral licensing. Typically, when a leader engages in moral licensing, it's his or her integrity that takes the biggest hit.

Early in my career, I was surprised to realize that, without meaning to and to their own detriment, some employers actually discourage behaving with integrity. Take the example of one law firm that stated, openly and frequently, that among its guiding principles were *teamwork* and *communication*—two honorable behaviors, to be certain. With those principles in mind, the firm encouraged—no, make that *urged*—its senior partners to mentor newer, younger partners. Again, a noble and understandable pursuit. After all, the senior partners had much wisdom and guidance to share with junior associates. As mentors, not only would they ensure the work quality of younger lawyers, but they would also create a bond, ensuring the associates' loyalty and longevity with the firm.

As a student of behavior and an executive coach, I applauded the law firm's intentions. But—and so many times, there is a but—the reality was that the senior partners' compensation was based entirely on billable hours. With such a compensation package, there was little incentive for senior lawyers to do the right thing. In fact, for them, mentoring was somewhat punitive, in that taking time to mentor meant taking away time for which they could have billed hours and been compensated.

In this instance, mentoring might have been valuable for the organization, but it was detrimental to the individual. For the partners, it was a genuine dilemma. And that is exactly how the slippery slope of foundering integrity is constructed. Instead of nurturing a climate of collaboration and teamwork, the firm had unwittingly created internal competition and silo behavior—much of which was interpreted as lack of integrity. Competition between departments is highly damaging to companies because it leads department heads to look out only for the interests of their part of the business. Resources are wasted. Client relations suffer. One major objective you should have when you apply behavior-based approaches to leadership is to create a corporate culture where leaders and followers work together in harmony to pursue your vision forward. It's not as difficult to do as you might think.

Let's look at another example that illustrates the importance of integrity as it applies to leadership. I work with the rising star of a small construction management company, Jack, who is, indeed, a jack-of-all-trades. Seemingly overnight, Jack's responsibilities have blossomed within the company. In a few short years, not only has he become a significant individual contributor, managing multiple accounts, but he is also the manager of a good-sized team and is the company's go-to guy for extraneous events and projects, which fall outside his job description. Jack has terrific potential and is a hard worker, and his devotion to this small company is undeniable. Yet, as a manager, he is failing. Not too long ago his team regarded him as unethical.

Let me point out that Jack doesn't actually lack integrity. He was *perceived* as lacking integrity. One specific complaint was that he didn't keep his commitments. When leaders do not keep their commitments, they are seen as unethical. So I looked more deeply and found that Jack wasn't delegating as he should. But why? Was he overworked? Was he unable to prioritize? Was the fault really his? I didn't believe so. Upon closer examination, I saw that Jack's compensation was not at all related to managing people or the many extraneous projects that landed on his plate. Jack's compensation was based on his performance as an individual contributor. He was paid for the number of *clients* he managed. With this bottom-line structure, Jack was destined to fail as a leader.

Managing people could not be a priority for him, because his performance was evaluated based on managing accounts. Clearly, part of Jack's compensation should have been based on the number of people he managed. I worked with the company's CEO to restructure Jack's incentives. Jack quickly understood and conformed to the readjusted expectations. When I followed up a few months later with a 360-degree interview process, Jack's integrity scores were significantly different. Why? Because as Jack was able to focus somewhat less on managing accounts and more on managing people, he began meeting his commitments. As he met his commitments, he was regarded as a person with integrity.

If it sounds simple, it's because it is: people do what they are paid to do. As mentioned earlier, people perform behaviors that are rewarded. I often strongly recommend to clients that they investigate and review their total rewards program—from total compensation to all the little perks their organizations offer people, including seemingly inconsequential perks such as public recognition and proximity and access to the leadership team.

Compensation packages are just one land mine in the integrity field. Let's not disregard the overblown sense of entitlement to which some leaders are prone. During a recent round of 360-degree interviews, I spoke with a law firm associate about her senior partner, Louis. When she gave Louis a low score for integrity, I asked her, as is my habit, to give a concrete example. She didn't hesitate: "He always keeps the most-desirable caseloads for himself."

In itself, this is hardly an appalling lapse of integrity; however, it does point to tiny incremental behaviors that can grow and, ultimately, backfire. In my experience, most leaders do not intend to behave without integrity. For them, the loss of integrity tends to happen incrementally. It starts with one little decision—one little temptation—like fudging a spreadsheet ("Just this one time!") or foisting undesirable work onto subordinates. The danger is that each bad behavior makes it easier to rationalize the next bad decision. Before long, cheating, which at one time may have given the leader at least a twinge of guilt, is done without a blink of the eye. And, just as we teach our children, the white lies and unethical behaviors pile up, becoming something much darker. The next thing you know, the leader is misrepresenting the entire balance sheet and, to cover his or her tracks, is telling bald-faced lies to the board of directors. One seemingly innocuous bad decision has irrevocably snowballed out of control.

Why integrity works

> The glue that holds all relationships together—
> including the relationship between the leader and
> the led is trust, and trust is based on integrity.
> —Brian Tracy

As noted, behaving with integrity—managing your company's reputation, as well as your own—is good for business.

When you behave with integrity, people know they can trust you—no doubt a benefit at any time but particularly beneficial during stressful times, when difficult business decisions must be made. Paul, the CEO of a midmarket company who had built up considerable "honesty capital" with his employees, is a good example. From his actions and communications over the years, Paul's employees knew him to be honest and ethical. During the recession of 2009—a stressful time in itself—the board of directors decided to divest of the company. At that point, Paul was able to use his honesty capital and open the lines of communication with his employees, who believed him and were calmed when he said, "You have nothing to worry about. We will ensure that the investor will take into account the well-being of our employees." This situation could have become a calamitous and detrimental event in the history of the company, but instead the employees were supportive and ended up working together to ensure a smooth transition.

When a leader behaves erratically, unpredictably, or unfairly, employees and colleagues become defensive. Instead of following, they construct walls and barriers to protect themselves. Just imagine how Paul's employees might have reacted had he been untrustworthy or inconsistent.

According to the Ethics Resource Center, a nonprofit organization working to be a catalyst in fostering *ethical* practices in individuals and institutions, "The most significant factor in ethical leadership is employees' perception of their leader's personal character. Leaders who demonstrate they are ethical people have a much greater impact on worker behavior than deliberate and visible efforts to promote ethics."

Note the word *perception*. As mentioned earlier, one happy consequence of my career choice is that I am almost always working with individuals who genuinely want to be better leaders. However, at times I work with strong leaders who have equally strong values but who aren't regarded as being particularly ethical. They may have integrity, but people don't realize it.

In their book *Firing Back*, Jeffrey Sonnenfeld and Andrew Ward write, "As a leader, you have to not only do the right thing, but be perceived to be doing the right thing. A consequence of seeking a leadership position is being put under intense public scrutiny, being held to high standards, and enhancing a reputation that is constantly under threat."

Nurturing integrity

> Men acquire a particular quality
> by constantly acting in a particular way.
> —Aristotle

At the end of the day, most of the executives I coach get high integrity ratings. Omar, a human resources professional, was particularly highly regarded. In a series of 360-degree interviews, coworkers described him as "a real Boy Scout—honest, loyal and true." From what I could observe, integrity comes easily and naturally to Omar. He seems to live by some code.

One day I finally asked his secret. After some prodding, he confessed, "It's pretty basic. I just try to live by the 'red-faced test.'" I must have looked pretty puzzled, because Omar quickly added, "You know, if I ever question whether I'm making the right decision, I ask myself whether I could tell my mom about the decision without being embarrassed— without getting red in the face."

A mentor from my early career put it another way: "With any questionable decision, ask yourself, *How would I feel about this being reported on the front page of the newspaper?*" In today's environment, I translate this into "How would I feel about this being spread through social media?"

Ethical behavior is easy to identify. Leaders with integrity are honest. They do what they say they're going to do. Their behavior is predictable. They behave with honor.

People occasionally waver, of course, in which case getting someone else's perspective can help keep the integrity "train" on the tracks. If I am working with an executive with a moral dilemma, we outline all the consequences, good and bad. Usually, these are questions that do not have a yes-or-no answer. There is often gray area. However, oftentimes a leader will realize just in asking the question what the correct course of action should be.

Based on thousands of 360-degree interviews and asking, "How would you rate this person on integrity, and how would you define integrity?" I've discovered some common dos and don'ts:

In the corporate world, leaders with high integrity *do* the following things:

- take blame and are quick to share credit
- do what they promise and tell the truth
- make decisions for the greater good (the organization)
- behave with dignity even when no one is looking
- act consistently and fairly
- are discreet and keep confidences

Leaders with high integrity *do not* do these things:

- gossip
- bend the rules to make things easier for themselves
- succumb to temptation
- rationalize their bad decisions or inappropriate behavior

Unlike other essential leadership behaviors, including empathy, self-stewardship, and self-awareness, the perception of integrity is built—or, really, accumulated—over a long period of time. However, what takes a lifetime to construct can be lost in an instant. That's why it's important to be mindful of your integrity and of behaviors that might lead people to think you are unethical and untrustworthy. In short, nurturing your integrity, guarding your reputation as an honest and ethical individual, is part of being a good leader.

Consider the example of NBC news anchor Brian Williams, once one of the most highly regarded journalists in the country. As he himself admitted, at some point, his ego overtook his common sense. Eventually, instead of telling the truth about his actual limited journalistic involvement in and proximity to historic events, he began claiming more participation, more involvement.

The truth, of course, caught up with him. Despite years of noteworthy and reliable reporting, Williams's misstep resulted in a near-instant fall from grace. He was suspended from his post and ultimately replaced.

Rebuilding integrity takes time; however, it is not impossible. The key is to develop and adhere to a personal PR plan, including (as quickly as practical) the following steps:

- acknowledging the mistake
- taking blame
- explaining what steps you'll take to repair the damage
- asking for understanding and allowing others time to recover and heal

And finally, at the risk of sounding simplistic, be kind—not just because it is the right thing to do but also because most people assume that the kinder you are, the more integrity you have. In the corporate world, you can be forgiven for a lot, provided that you show vulnerability and humility, communicate clearly, and are kind. I am not advocating a popularity contest in which you try to make everyone like you. As a leader, that is impossible. In fact, if everyone likes you and you have no opposing opinions or dissent, then you are probably not exhibiting managerial courage and making tough calls.

Remember, too, that recovering from a loss (even a perceived loss) of integrity will take time. I once worked with an executive who learned that—for right or wrong—his employees didn't feel that he had high integrity. He was devastated but developed a personal plan to develop and display personal integrity. The road was long and difficult, but he persisted for fourteen months, at the end of which I interviewed some of my original 360-degree feedback responders. The news was gratifying and satisfying. His efforts had paid off; he had indeed succeeded in changing the perception of his integrity for the better.

I asked Taylor, the chief executive I told you about at the beginning of this chapter, how he coped with the pressure of doing his job and maintaining his integrity. "For me," he said, "it has always been pretty simple. I only worry about doing my job well. I never worry about losing it. I guess that keeps me on the right path."

Taylor was secure. He had no fear. And he always followed the basic dos and don'ts of ethical leadership.

Leadership roundup

Admittedly, empathy, humility, and integrity are rather abstract human constructs. You can't see or touch them. In a way, self-awareness and self-control are easier to grasp. We know that if we think about ourselves and how we interact with the larger world, we're at least a little self-aware. We know that if we get mad but keep our cool, we're exercising self-control. Ditto if we don't order that delicious sundae after a big meal at a restaurant. But even in the abstract the devil is in the details. Integrity is delicate, like an orchid. It needs tender, loving care to survive in the sometimes rough-and-tumble day-to-day course of business.

- Integrity plays a vital part in the image you project to your superiors, colleagues, and subordinates. Always do what you say you'll do, and do it when you say you will.
- Respect and be kind to teammates. Foster a culture of collaboration. Positive work environments breed the perception that you are a person of integrity. Leaders working within negative corporate environments are often viewed as unethical and lacking integrity. Therefore, teamwork and harmony matter on a deeper level than simply boosting the company's bottom line.

- Consistency in your behavior matters. If you're seen as erratic, lacking self-control, failing to understand or care, and just out for yourself, you'll be seen as lacking integrity. Conversely, the opposite is true if you demonstrate positive behaviors, many of which translate into perceived integrity.
- Give credit to others when it is merited. Don't be afraid to take the blame if something goes wrong and it's even remotely your fault.
- Treat people with kindness, honesty, and fairness even if you have nothing to gain.

Chapter 7

Personal Stewardship

Spirit. Mind. Body.
—The Young Men's Christian Association (YMCA)

During an interview as a dental school applicant, my daughter Katrina was asked, "How do you handle stress?" In context, the question was pretty expected. The interviewer likely had in mind that dentistry, with its unusual combination of medical care plus small-business management, is acknowledged to be one of the more stressful professions. My daughter's response, though, may have been less expected: "I believe in mind, body, and spirit balance," she responded. "I'm intellectually active with school, I'm physically active with dance and running, and I stay spiritually active with my church."

Phew. Upon hearing this story, I have to admit that my first response was relief! It turns out that, all those years, Katrina had been listening to me after all! But when I look at her response from a coaching perspective, I also appreciate the precision of her response.

Think about it. The best leaders—in personal and in professional settings—take care of themselves physically, intellectually, and spiritually. And while we want those three elements to remain in balance, the reality is that, for most of us, the goal isn't so much well balanced as well juggled. Each of the three balls must be kept in play, despite the fact that each is on its own trajectory. The balls are never all on the same level. Sometimes, the best we can hope for is that none of the balls falls and crashes to the floor!

I am not a life coach; my coaching is leadership and business oriented. However, the more I work with executives and professionals, the more clearly I recognize the relationship between taking care of oneself (i.e., personal stewardship) and taking care of a business. How can leaders attend to the needs of others or, indeed, a business if they are unable to attend to themselves?

In seminars, I often ask participants, "Are the best leaders healthy?" At first, people are puzzled. It's obviously not a question they routinely consider. Within seconds, though, everyone will begin nodding. Yes, as they think about it, they all agree: the best leaders are healthy.

But are all the best leaders healthy? Of course not. It's a trick question. Leaders aren't superheroes. Despite their achievements, accolades, expertise, and laurels, leaders are susceptible to the same physical ills, shortcomings, and weaknesses as the rest of us. But here's the difference: effective leaders address these issues. While they may not be perfectly healthy and may not get perfectly clean bills of health from their physicians, they *are* health conscious. They recognize the need to take care of themselves. Moreover, they make self-care—self-stewardship—a priority. Just as they would address business matters with a sense of urgency, effective leaders deal with health issues quickly and consistently.

The three-legged stool

> People go through three conversions: their head,
> their heart, and their pocketbook. Unfortunately,
> not all at the same time.
> —Martin Luther (1483–1546)

The way I see it, personal stewardship is a three-legged stool, consisting of physical, emotional, and spiritual components. Your life, your relationships, your work—they all rest on this stool. If one leg is slightly shorter or not well fastened or missing the glide at the bottom, the stool may wobble annoyingly or, under the pressure of weight, tumble over altogether. And like the wobbly stool that can't be effectively propped up with a sugar packet or folded-up paper napkin, the unbalanced leader can't be propped up with a simple, one-time fix.

Personal stewardship cannot be faked. A leader might be able to *pretend* to be humble or empathetic; indeed, as an executive coach, I often encourage leaders to perform behaviors such as humility or empathy until the behaviors come naturally. Personal stewardship, however, cannot be feigned. And in many ways, it can't be coached. Personal stewardship must be addressed deliberately and regularly on a very individual and personal level.

Plenty of leaders live with diabetes or depression. Many battle weight issues or have crises of faith. They are human, with health issues of the body, mind, and spirit. I work with a lawyer, Ben, who confided in me that, for most of his adult life, he has battled depression. To his credit, Ben followed his doctor's orders and began a course of antidepressants. And even more to his credit, when the results of a 360-degree interview indicated that his coworkers found his behavior to be erratic, he went back to his physician to determine whether the prescribed medicine was working as it should.

A successful leader recognizes that being an effective manager requires self-care. Successful leaders seek treatment. They take required medication as prescribed. They eat properly. They exercise. They take care of their spirits.

As problem solvers, the most successful professionals take the same drive they apply to their business and apply it to their personal lives. When they detect an issue, they seek a solution. If their marriage is going bad, they get marital counseling. When a toothache crops up, they don't let it fester for days; they call the dentist.

Simply put, in their efforts to lead others, the best and most effective leaders don't neglect *themselves*, any more than they neglect their businesses. Like my daughter the dental student, they are their own personal stewards, tending to body, mind, and spirit.

Your personal stewardship, or the lack thereof, will be noticed. While it's an area that many leaders tend to ignore, it truly is behavioral in nature. Let's take a close look at the three legs of the personal stewardship stool.

Leg 1: Body

> To keep the body in good health is a duty ...
> otherwise we shall not be able to keep our mind strong and clear.
> —Buddha

When in the midst of executive coaching I eventually address the behavior of physical stewardship, most managers light up. At last! Of all the behaviors of successful leaders, this is one they can immediately grasp! On some level, each of us can. This is the stuff thrown at us every day. In grocery store checkout lines, on TV news shows, even on fast-food menus, we are bombarded with messages about improving our health, watching our weight, counting calories, brightening our smiles, and toning our abs. This behavior is the most visually obvious: if you work out and eat properly, people can tell. Making a favorable impression, though, is the least of the reasons to take care of one's physical body.

The body is just one leg of the three-legged personal-stewardship stool, but it's essential, involving taking care of your physical body through exercise, nutrition, and other actions to prevent disease. Of the three legs, body is the most touted and most popular—and not just among executives. Celebrities, athletes, and even US presidents can be seen on the evening news working out or discussing their nutrition choices.

President Ford skied and played tennis and golf. President Obama runs, works out, and plays golf and basketball. President George W. Bush was an avid runner and mountain biker throughout his presidency. Physical fitness isn't just a modern trend among US presidents—President Theodore (Teddy) Roosevelt wrestled, boxed, fenced, rock climbed, practiced jujitsu, played tennis, rode horseback, and hiked! Do you exercise regularly? If so, what's your favorite form of exercise? Regular exercise can actually become healthfully addictive. In other words, we don't feel right if we don't get our usual amount of exercise. The body physically needs it, but we have to get started. Some studies say that it takes up to six weeks to condition ourselves to a new exercise program. If we make it that long, we'll likely stick with it. That's a good thing! And guess what. It takes disciplined self-control to make it happen.

Physical fitness, of course, can be easily neglected. We all have been guilty of the "tomorrow syndrome." *The gym was closed when I got off work; I'll do it tomorrow. My knees hurt today; I'll go for a run tomorrow. The office was crazy today; I'll make time for exercise tomorrow.* However, no American can claim unawareness of the benefits of physical fitness. As I said before, we are all but bombarded by it. We hear that proper nutrition helps us lead longer and healthier lives. We're told that exercise helps prevent cognitive decline and increases productivity. In fact, we don't even need to be told. When we exercise regularly, we experience the positive impacts quite quickly. If we're healthy of body, it stands to reason we'll be healthy of mind. If we're happy and fit, it also stands to reason that we may well live longer than if we are unhappy and in poor health.

Nonetheless, despite study after study showing the benefits of physical health and nutrition, we still see people—potential leaders—neglecting their health. And not just in obvious ways, like overindulging, but also in less obvious ways, like failing to follow doctors' orders. Did you know, for example, that one in five new prescriptions goes unfilled?

Unless put into action, though, *knowledge* of physical fitness is useless. It must be acted upon, and how you approach the physical aspect of personal stewardship is up to you. One fine example is Dorothy, a fifty-something client with a demanding job in a large organization. Dorothy is a manager, a physician, and a teacher. She's a parent, a spouse, and an active church member. Suffice to say, Dorothy's schedule is *overflowing*. Somehow, though, she manages to keep all three legs of her personal-stewardship stool grounded—all while being one of the most energetic people I know. When I asked Dorothy about it, she said, "I don't always feel *balanced*. I often feel, in fact, that I'm not doing all I should. So, at the end of every week, I make a point of looking back and seeing where I fell short. Did I eat well? Did I take the elevator when I could have taken the stairs? Did I say no to the extra glass of wine? For me, it's the little things. All week long I have plenty of *opportunities* to make good decisions. I just have to be sure I *actually make* those decisions."

"Last night, for example," Dorothy continued, "I spent last night on the floor of my church, with some of our area's homeless. I feel good about the work I did there. It fed my spirit. So then, I could go on and work out at the gym—to take care of my physical self."

The ties between a healthy body and effective leadership are undeniable. A manager who isn't physically healthy, for whatever reason, often isn't present or able to manage his or her responsibilities. A manager who doesn't tend to his or her physical body might find it hard to be a role model and to attract followers.

Tending to the physical body needn't be publicized. It can be a very private, personal affair. In fact, I'd argue that it's pointless for an executive to work out obsessively and post his or her progress for all the world to see on Facebook. Likewise, there's little to be gained by hopping on the latest diet fad and boring people with the details of your every meal. Like the other behaviors discussed in this book, personal stewardship is a choice, but it's a highly personal choice. It needn't be public, and it needn't be all-consuming. Health consciousness is for *you*—not for anyone else.

I once worked with a CEO, Jason, who seemed to have it all. Widely admired and highly regarded, health consciousness seemed to come naturally to him. As we worked together, though, Jason confided that he suffered from panic attacks. If he hadn't told me, I never would have guessed. But that's because he addressed the issue head-on. Jason wasn't ashamed. He went to a therapist and sought treatment. He took care of himself. And by doing so, in addition to living a healthier life, he could do his job and lead more effectively.

Your physical body is important. It's your physical essence, your visible form for the intangible mind and soul that constitute who you truly are as a unique human being. It pays dividends to take care of your body. At the risk of sounding like a broken record, I'm going to state the obvious: diet and nutrition, regular exercise, weight management, getting enough sleep, and following your doctor's orders are all essential parts of the first leg of your personal-stewardship stool.

Leg 2: Mind

> Leadership and learning are indispensable to each other.
> —John Fitzgerald Kennedy

A few years ago, I found a current issue of *Popular Mechanics* in the stack of mail at home. Odd, yes, but I was only mildly puzzled. Surely it had been misdelivered. I'm a leadership and business coach, my husband is an architect, and our daughters are, well, not remotely interested in what's under the hood of a car. None of us is the *Popular Mechanics* sort.

Upon closer examination, however, I saw that the magazine was plainly and accurately addressed to our home. The plot thickened as I realized the magazine was addressed to my husband, Bill. I was mystified but came up with a couple of plausible explanations. Perhaps I was holding a marketing effort gone awry. Perhaps it was one of those free-with-purchase kind of situations. I was ready to dismiss it, concluding that Bill probably had no idea he was now a *Popular Mechanics* subscriber. Still, just to be sure, I mentioned it. "Out of curiosity, this isn't yours, is it?" I asked.

"Oh," he responded, somewhat vaguely, "yes, I subscribed."

As Bill's wife, I've always appreciated his sense of whimsy and curiosity, but as a behaviorist, I should have appreciated his unexpected deviation from *National Geographic* and *Harvard Business Review*. Bill's behavior is consistent with that of the most successful leaders. His intellectual curiosity expands well outside the walls of his area of expertise. Deliberate or not, he's keeping his mind sharp and well exercised—even if his wife, the behaviorist, didn't immediately recognize it!

A well-known phenomenon among American executives is that as they ascend the ladder and assume more and more management responsibilities, they perform less of the tactical work upon which their careers were based. And as essential as management is, it is no replacement for the mental acuity needed to, for example, perform neurosurgery, draft architectural plans, or solve engineering problems.

Great leaders challenge themselves. They keep their minds well exercised—at levels expected and not. They remain well informed—in ways expected and not. I work with many who, for reasons known only to them, have learned later in life to fly planes or to speak a second language. Keeping a mind keen and alert doesn't require these extremes, though, delightful as they may be. The point is to do *something*, to keep *learning*, to keep exercising your mind just as you exercise your body.

When I first struck out on my own as a leadership consultant, I was understandably anxious. In my previous position in a large corporation, I'd been able to rely on others to manage certain details that fell outside my area of expertise. As a self-employed consultant, though, all the details were on me, and I had genuine self-doubts. Could I manage spreadsheets? Administer assessments? Deal with essential bookkeeping and purchasing? And what in the world would I do without a supportive IT department at the end of the hall? It didn't take long, though. The more I stretched my mind and the more tasks I tackled, the more I grew. I felt my mind stretching in ways it hadn't since my early career. I felt sharp, aware, and, ultimately, on top of things. And while I'm still no IT expert, I've had the satisfaction of learning that I'm actually good at many things outside my so-called area of expertise!

You don't need to quit your job and start your own company to develop this second leg of your personal-stewardship stool. Successful leaders read the paper, staying aware of news at the local, national, and international level. Many stimulate their minds by following politics; others, by learning new software applications or teaching themselves how to code. Comic and former talk show host Jay Leno is equally well known for collecting and restoring old cars. I work with one tenacious client who sharpens his mind by checking in on his kids' homework, tackling their calculus problems as if they were his own.

Like the other two legs of the personal-stewardship stool, this one can be easily overlooked. After all, most successful leaders have already worked, earlier in their careers, at building their minds. They attended school, took the right classes, aimed for the right scores, and so on. As students, many were overachievers. The problem arises, however, in what can be an inevitable tendency to let learning lapse.

Learning—exercising the mind—should be a lifelong commitment and not merely because of the obvious benefits of improved memory, mental acuity, and a more complete knowledge base. Learning keeps a leader sharp and informed. Keeping the mind sharp can be as consuming as learning to fly a plane or as simple as going to the movies and engaging in conversations with friends.

Many of my clients even find they can combine the first and second legs of the stool: physical and mental. For example, a client who rock climbs says that the mental focus and physical demands are a perfect escape. Another attends ballroom dancing classes on the weekend with her husband. In addition to the obvious physical exercise, she's challenged by memorizing unfamiliar dance moves.

The goal here is to do something new, something perhaps out of your comfort zone and certainly outside your area of expertise. I hope you'll pardon me for mentioning George W. Bush for a second time in this chapter, as I am not a particularly political creature; however, he is a fascinating role model. No longer a sitting US president, he has taken up painting and has even staged an art exhibit of his portraits of world leaders, including his father, George H. W. Bush. Former British prime minister Winston Churchill was also an artist.

Not quite the same thing as subscribing to *Popular Mechanics*, but you get the point. Keep learning. Keep trying new things. Strengthen that second leg of the stool at every opportunity.

The following activities are among the many ways to exercise mental well-being:

- reading
- going to the movies—particularly ones that wouldn't be on your usual radar
- using both sides of the brain
- staying informed (internally, locally, nationally, globally)
- continuing to learn
- opening the mind through acupressure, massage therapy, or meditation
- using brain-building apps

- listening to podcasts
- improving your grammar or vocabulary
- engaging in logical arguments and debates, making points and counterpoints

Leg 3: Spirit

> Knowledge is only one half. Faith is the other.
> —Novalis

And now we come to the third leg of the personal-stewardship stool: *spirit*.

Of all the desirable leadership behaviors, this is the one most fraught with tension. When the topic arises, leaders who are regular churchgoers feel vindicated. Those who aren't feel judged. Again, I'm not a life coach. I'm a behaviorist. And although I have a deep faith and attribute much of my personal success to my faith, I don't presume that my way is the only way.

What I do know is that individuals who tend to their spirits—whether by traditional (organized religion) or untraditional means—are more balanced and effective leaders.

From my observations, spirit is the most overlooked leg of the personal-stewardship stool. And not only do I see this as detrimental to an individual's leadership, but it also makes me sad to see individuals neglect their souls—their spirits.

I work with Thomas, the CEO of a technology company, who is an avowed and outspoken atheist, adamant in his nonbelief. Thomas claims that he can't believe in anything that he can't see, that he can't prove. We've worked together for many years, so we're comfortable discussing his faith, or lack thereof. For his part, Thomas doesn't see the value of feeding his spirit. For my part, I enjoy the debate. (Perhaps I'm indulging my need for mental exercise with our discussions!)

I enjoy pointing out how much easier it is to be an atheist than to have faith. I like poking holes in Thomas's arguments and waiting to see his reaction. Eventually, though, I gave up the debate and told Thomas that if he can't have faith, he needs to find something—anything—about which he is passionate. I finally asked, "What feeds your spirit? What is the one thing that if taken from you would devastate you?" Initially, Thomas was stymied. To be truthful, nothing much fazes him, but then he told me about a project he's working on. The project has nothing to do with work and everything to do with his family. Thomas is working with his grandchildren to self-publish a children's book. The project, the process, and even the telling of it bring him unimaginable joy. *This* is what feeds Thomas's soul. Clearly, this is where Thomas should devote more time and effort to tend to his spirit.

My soul is nourished through church and prayer and meditation. But just as plainly, I feed my spirit with family time and service work. But that's me. You know what works for you. I know many CEOs who pause during the workday or before a meal to offer a prayer. For you, nourishing your spirit may be hiking through the woods or fly-fishing. I met with a medical professional this week who strolls through an art gallery when she finds her spirit is lagging. Something about interpreting and appreciating the paintings feeds her spirit.

For you, the choice may not even be an action. It may be the seashell kept on your desk that reminds you of a special trip or a photo of your grandparents.

A few years back, when my girls were younger and family time was hard to come by, my husband insisted on doing all our yard work himself. He mowed; he fertilized; he raked; he trimmed. And frankly, it irritated me. While we couldn't easily afford a lawn service, to me it would be worth the cost so that we could spend more time together as a family. After all, Bill was working overtime, every day and every week, to build his business. He had little time to spare. I felt strongly that when he was home, he should be available to us—his wife and children.

Looking back, I was pretty outspoken about it, pushing Bill hard to relinquish his status as the yard guy. I pointed out that the girls were young and needed our attention. I pointed out that before long they'd be old enough to drive and spend more time away from us. *Now* was the time for us to make sacrifices to be with them. I thought he was being bullheaded. How could he not get his priorities straight?

Eventually, though, I observed and accepted that doing that physical work out in the sun restored his soul. And when I thought about it, Bill wasn't working in isolation. Not at all. While he pushed the mowers, the girls weren't far behind. They'd hover and buzz and dance around him, so much so that I could have been envious—if it hadn't been obvious how soul satisfying it was, to both him and the girls. The chore of yard work fed Bill's soul and, in an unexpected way, brought our family closer together.

On occasion, I have the pleasure of working with individuals who plainly are already gifted leaders. When I have such an opportunity, I always pose the same question: "What makes you so successful?" So far, the answer has never been education or training or even opportunity. Without fail, the answer is more spiritually related—"my family" or "my faith" or sometimes "I'm blessed."

These are the leaders who well know how to nourish their souls.

Striking a balance

> The first wealth is health.
> —Ralph Waldo Emerson

Remember your very first boss? Your first real manager? Think of all the people you've worked with and worked for. Think of the ones you've admired. I don't need to tell you: you know from personal experience that people want to follow well-balanced leaders. However, in the real world, there's no way a person can be expected to do justice to all three aspects of self-care—physical, mental, and spiritual—on a daily basis.

Outside of a monastery, I don't know how anyone could devote equal time on a daily basis to all aspects of self-care. I certainly can't. But what I am able to do—and what you can as well—is look beyond the day and look at seven-day increments. About once a week I ask myself, *Where have I fallen short? Did I spend too little time with family? Did I make time for exercise? Where do I need to put more effort?* If at the beginning of the week I didn't focus on my work, I make up for it on the weekend.

I also look for trade-offs. If I feel I am neglecting my family or not getting enough exercise, I might have to outsource other time-consuming tasks. When my girls were young, for example, I decided to pay someone to help with housework. It was a difficult and expensive decision. Money was tight, and I certainly knew how to keep a clean house, but the price of me doing it meant less family time. So we tightened our belts, hired some help, and got the family time we needed.

Some of my clients outsource other chores. They subcontract what is not essential, paying to have their lawns mowed, houses cleaned, dry cleaning delivered. Yes, they're paying a financial price, but it's all to avoid paying in other ways. They're wise enough to realize that you can't have a perfect marriage, perfect children, a perfect career, a perfect financial situation, a perfect house, and perfect health all at the same time. Eventually, something has to give. And eventually, something—physically, mentally, or spiritually—will end up suffering.

Businesses can make similar decisions. For example, instead of putting more demands on yourself and your staff for tasks like event planning or specialized marketing projects, you can pay to have someone else manage those tasks, leaving you more time and opportunities to address other priorities.

Finally, one last observation: *don't overlook the value of friendship.* Particularly early in our careers, as we focus on climbing ladders and building marriages and starting families, friendships can fall by the wayside. There is, however, no substitute for good friends outside of work and family. Friendships feed the soul and, according to many surveys, are key to happiness.

Workaholics

Although my expertise lies in helping leaders be effective at work, I'm the first to acknowledge that too much work takes a tremendous toll on a person—physically, mentally, and spiritually.

Ironically, in my experience, it's more often the followers who are workaholics, rather than the leaders. Individuals who have risen to the rank of CEO have often risen above the need to prove themselves. Sadly, though, many who aspire to lead are inefficient, working more than they need to—either to catch up or impress. For others, it's almost an addiction—to fill a void or to get a high from recognition.

If you're reading this book, you're probably ambitious. You're probably into continuous self-improvement, so I'm not asking you to work less (on yourself or on your job). I'm asking you to ask yourself why you do it. What is it costing you? Is there anything you can do about it? Is it possible you can manipulate your schedule and shape your priorities so you don't get burned out in any particular area?

Look to your CEO. Is he or she putting in as many hours as you are? Most of the time, the answer I hear is no. And if that's the case, you have to ask yourself why. Effective leaders are better balanced. They figure out the formula. They exert energy in other directions and efficiently. They tend to themselves—physically, mentally, and spiritually.

As should you.

Leadership roundup

Personal stewardship is a highly private pursuit, and yet it does come into visible play when you lead a company. The proverbial fishbowl pertains more here than perhaps in any other aspect of behavioral leadership besides self-control. If you lack self-control, people will notice. And fast! If you lack a firm belief in your own personal stewardship, people will notice, though not as fast as they will if you blow your stack in a board meeting. Personal stewardship should be part of your self-awareness as a person and as a leader. If you don't take care of yourself, nobody else will.

- Steady personal stewardship is good for your business and for your personal life. Never negate the power of happiness and positive thinking that can come as a benefit from being a good personal steward.
- There are three legs to the personal-stewardship stool—body, mind, and spirit. All should receive as much attention as possible.
- Time management for personal stewardship can become difficult for busy leaders. Don't feel badly about doing a bit of a juggling act. If you have time for only working out at the gym and not playing a game of chess with a friend, consider it a trade-off for the week. The important thing to do is find a balance between the three legs of the personal stewardship stool and the amount of time you have.
- Working too hard (being a workaholic) can derail your personal life and career. There is more to life than work.

Chapter 8

Communication

The problem with communication is the illusion that is has occurred.
—George Bernard Shaw

When a large manufacturing company ousted its tough-talking but ineffective president, it brought in Elsa, an outsider, to turn the business around. Elsa had her work cut out for her: the company had been foundering for years and was verging on bankruptcy. Goals weren't being met, profit margins were razor thin, and, particularly challenging for Elsa, the company—like so many in the industry—was heavily male dominated.

Elsa had been hired because of her proven track record managing the financial and operational aspects of another company. I believe her greatest value, however, was a strength she didn't recognize in herself: Elsa was a gifted communicator.

She innately understood the importance of clear, frequent, and thoughtful communications. It was her choice to request my services to ensure that she did not stumble as she began taking the necessary change-management and cultural-transformation steps.

I noticed right away that people gravitated toward Elsa. She had a knack for knowing exactly how to project her communication, whether written or face-to-face, to virtually any audience. The feedback I got during her

360-degree interviews described someone who clearly and consistently articulated her expectations. One of her direct reports told me, "I know exactly what she's asking for without having to probe much. If she's not sure that she communicated well—and that is a rare phenomenon—she will check for understanding by asking me questions and ensuring that I know exactly what needs to be accomplished." Elsa was equally effective in written communications, applying a warm, professional tone as she clearly stated her requests, the parameters, and the timelines.

Elsa could also work a crowd, inspiring her audience by painting a beautiful picture of where she saw the business in the future and then explaining the steps to get there. Thinking even bigger, Elsa instituted a well-considered rewards system to motivate the right behaviors and provide incentives correlated with stated objectives, thus ensuring the success of the overall organization.

Elsa got the job because of her considerable business acumen, education, and experience, but in the end, it was her gift for communication that allowed her to transform the organization and lay the groundwork for its success.

Communication—*effective* communication—is undeniably essential to a successful leader. Self-awareness requires internal communication, and external communication is needed to fully appreciate how we are perceived. Hence, the 360-degree feedback process is a powerful tool in assisting leaders in their efforts to be more self-aware. Likewise, internal (the self) and external (the larger world) communication goes on every day when it comes to self-control, empathy, humility, and integrity. Each component of the behavioral approach to executive leadership requires a high degree of effective communication, whether verbal, written, or even physical. (Behaviorists and researchers agree that a large percentage of communication isn't verbal at all.)

Ironically, I find that communication presents a big stumbling block for many leaders. They think they're getting the message across, but they're not being as clear as they could be. Other things get in the way as well. Perhaps the followers are afraid of the leader, or they think he or she lacks integrity. Perhaps the leader has unrealistic expectation or is erratic and childish. All these things will interfere with good communication that leads to harmonious and efficient businesses.

Let's face it: leaders like Elsa are uncommon, and ineffective communication is pervasive. We all have a tendency to believe that as long we are speaking a common language, we are communicating effectively, but really nothing could be further from the truth. Far from accurate, that perspective, for a leader, is narrow-minded if not downright dangerous. People filter what they hear. It's like how witnesses to a car wreck or a mugging will almost always see things differently from one another. Likewise, two people can receive the same message but take something different away from it. How does a leader ensure that what he or she says and writes is universally understood throughout the company? Repeating the message and asking individuals the right questions can help. Frequency of communication is important.

Years ago, I worked with a large American corporation that had acquired another fairly large company headquartered in Canada. Staff and administration from both companies were to be retained, and to ensure a smooth transition, a number of executive meetings between the American president and the Canadian president were vital. In one of the initial meetings, the American president asked a routine question about the status of some of the Canadian accounts. The Canadian president quickly said there was nothing to worry about. The American pressed further, asking to see the documentation and legal agreements that would clearly delineate the account status. The Canadian again said, "It's okay. This is not a problem." As the two parried, with one continuing to ask the same question and the other continuing to provide the same answer, tension mounted. Despite each saying exactly what he meant, the two were not getting each other at all.

When we finally took a break, I spoke to the American president, saying that perhaps the two of them weren't really understanding what the other was saying. At first, he was taken aback. "That's ridiculous," he said. "He's Canadian. He's just like us. He speaks English. He knows what I'm saying." But then, as we discussed the situation further, he acknowledged that his approach wasn't working, and we came up with a quick strategy. Upon returning from the break, the American president looked to his Canadian counterpart and humbly said, "I'm not sure what you mean when you say, 'This is not a problem.' Can you help me understand?" The Canadian president then immediately and fully answered the question to the American president's satisfaction.

I am baffled by the seeming lack of executive or managerial courage in communication. The best leaders have the courage and humility to check for understanding whether it is theirs or that of the person they're talking to. Likewise, they have the humility to admit when they may not understand what someone else is trying to communicate.

Effective communication isn't only an individual responsibility; it's a corporate one as well. As one might predict, effective communication leads to improved productivity, but it is also valuable from a recruiting and employee-retention perspective. One study has found that as many as 85 percent of employees are dissatisfied with workplace communications. And another sizable percentage, 81 percent, would rather join a company that values open communication than one that offers perks including free food and gym memberships.

A huge amount of my time as an executive coach is spent interpreting. I am fluent in four languages and, as such, am accustomed to translating for other people, but the interpreting I'm talking about now is for boards of directors, employees, colleagues, bosses, and sometimes even clients who all speak a common language but don't understand one another. I am constantly urging clients to interpret for themselves: Are you sure you said it that way? What words were you using? Are you certain this person meant that? Is it possible he or she meant something else?

Plainly put, speaking is not the same as communicating. I've written some of this book at my neighborhood Starbucks, and since I'm a regular, it's pretty easy for me to navigate the queue, place my order, flash my Starbucks app, move along to the next station, and retrieve my "tall, nonfat, vanilla latte."

Consider, though, the person who stood in line in front of me one morning who plainly was not so familiar with the language of Starbucks. Although the baristas were speaking English, I sensed that this first-time customer was confused and intimidated. I could only imagine what was running through her mind: *What does* grande *mean? Don't they have a size medium? What's the difference between nonfat and low fat? Why do I have to walk to another counter to get my drink? Am I the only person who isn't smart enough to know how to order a simple cup of coffee? Maybe I'll just have water.*

It's not my intent to pick on Starbucks, of course. My point is that *speaking* a common language (English) isn't the same as being *understood*. Elsa, mentioned at the beginning of this chapter, understood that instinctively. With a few tweaks here and there, she could refine her communication skills to near perfection.

To inspire and to motivate, a leader must communicate thoughtfully and intentionally with

- clarity,
- passion,
- vision and strategy,
- frequency, and
- shared objectives.

Each of these qualities is essential to effective communication. In the absence of clarity, we find conflict. A lack of passion leads to apathy and complacency. In the absence of vision and strategy, you have a workplace in chaos and confusion. Without frequency, your followers lose focus and waste energy on worry. And without shared objectives, you have inefficiency and suboptimization.

Clarity

> The less people know, the more they yell.
> —Seth Godin

While it may seem obvious, clarity of the message is the most important consideration when it comes to communicating. As I said, many leaders are under the mistaken impression that they're doing just fine as communicators. Let's take a look at an innocent goof that my client and friend Chris shared with me regarding his former manager. The manager was very professional, very buttoned-up, and very pleasant but also very detached. One Tuesday afternoon, the manager sent her team the following e-mail: "Plan to attend a *mandatory* meeting in the conference room Thursday at 2 p.m."

That was it. No details. No explanation. No verbal communication to key individuals to fill them in. Pretty much just a digital demand for a command performance.

As Chris remembers, while there wasn't sufficient time for anyone to get to the bottom of the reason for the meeting, there was ample time for self-exploration, during which every individual on the team concluded that he or she had done something wrong. "None of us knew what was going on. I honestly couldn't tell whether the company was going out of business or whether I had eaten lunch at my desk one too many times," says Chris.

After a day and a half of dread and speculation—a day and a half during which productivity and efficiency plummeted—the team silently trooped, single file, into the conference room, borderline panicked. As they guardedly took their seats, the manager said, "Thank you for coming. You've all been working really hard, so now, we're all going bowling."

You can imagine how the team felt. *Bowling? She sent us all into a tailspin so she could take us bowling?* At this point, going out and having fun was the last thing anyone wanted to do. While the manager was surely well intentioned, her plan backfired. Her failure to communicate clearly and openly resulted in personal anxiety, workplace inefficiency, and even conflicts and finger-pointing within her team—the *exact opposite* of what she had hoped to accomplish with a bowling outing!

Communicating with clarity requires three elements:

- being open and honest
- using understandable words and shared vernacular
- taking time to communicate well

Notice that these three requirements would be impossible without self-awareness, empathy, humility, and integrity. To carry out each of these three positive behaviors, one must have a talent for communication that exceeds that of most individuals. Yet, as a leader, you are not like most individuals. You're special. That's why you're in a leadership position. It pays to be aware of just how important communication is to your business—to your employees, your vendors, and your customers.

A *lack* of clarity results in conflict and misunderstanding—just as happened in Chris's workplace—which is then compounded when followers feel too intimidated to ask their leader for clarification. No one wants to be the one to raise his or her hand and say, "I don't understand what you are saying," because we assume that we should comprehend, even when we haven't been provided with sufficient information (background, details, lead time, and so on, i.e., *communication*) to do so.

President Ronald Reagan is often referred to as "the Great Communicator." Some of that, no doubt, is because of his attitude and acting ability, but how do you explain an admittedly older president attracting young voters in droves, revitalizing the Republican Party? When Reagan died in 2004, Lou Cannon described Reagan's gift for *clear communications*: "Reagan became the great communicator because he stood for something. In 1980, when Reagan ran for president, he talked more about issues than any presidential candidate had in years. He talked about building up the defense budget, cutting taxes and balancing the budget … [H]e talked about substance. But he kept his message basic and simple and on mainstream American concerns."

Clients will often tell me about frustrating and confusing business conversations. To make sure I understand the situation, they'll articulate their concerns and describe their thoughts and questions in great detail—to me. When I ask, "Well, did you say that [to the other person]?" they'll usually respond somewhat sheepishly, "No, I did not. I didn't want to stand out. I didn't want to look stupid for asking. I didn't want them to get impatient with me."

Plainly, *empathy*, discussed earlier in this book, is a component of effective communication. In other words, to communicate with our constituents, we have to understand their perspective, their education, their culture. If we really want to communicate clearly, we must understand our audience and speak their language—just like an interpreter at the United Nations. If you have traveled to a foreign country, I suspect you researched some key phrases or words to ensure that you would be able to make yourself understood. It's obvious. So shouldn't you make that same basic effort to make yourself clear in day-to-day business communications?

Muddled, unclear, and confusing communication is particularly prevalent in the technology world, which has its own jargon of unfamiliar English vocabulary and acronyms. An intelligent and successful client of mine from the retail industry, Samuel, met with a successful partner in the tech industry. My client—educated as he is—described the experience as intimidating. He simply didn't understand the language being spoken. Samuel had to remind himself that he too is a successful business leader, and he walked away from the uncomfortable experience determined to never make anyone else feel the same way.

Do you deliberately use lofty or obscure language to sound more intelligent or informed? That doesn't make you a great leader. It means you are being unclear. It means you are causing conflict. It means you are confusing your audience and sometimes even shaming them. The best leaders act as their own interpreters—they don't put the burden of understanding on the listener.

Another common mistake for leaders is to use shorthand in internal communications. I once worked with Jane, a manager in a bustling marketing agency. Jane was brilliant—communicating clearly and persuasively with clients while playing a key role in writing memorable, effective, and often hilarious marketing messages. Her internal communications, however, fell flat.

The 360-degree interviews I conducted with her peers revealed that Jane was "cryptic" in her e-mail communications, leaving recipients uncertain about what she really wanted. For example, Jane might forward a link to an industry news article to a direct report, who then had to decide if the link was merely an FYI or something to act upon. Even when Jane did include instructions in her e-mails or communications, she was curt, forcing the recipients to come back to her and ask her to elaborate with more direction, intent, or details.

One day, as Jane breezed past an employee's desk, she said, "You need to tidy up your desk."

With no chance to respond, the employee interpreted this as "You are a slob. Your desk is a mess. You need to do something about it—immediately—or you risk facing severe consequences."

But Jane didn't mean to come across as harsh. What she'd been hoping to communicate was "A client will be touring our offices later today. I'd like to make a great impression, so I'm asking everyone to take a minute or two to help tidy up. Thanks—I'm sure you understand."

Plainly, the employee *didn't* understand. And the reason is simple: Jane didn't communicate with clarity. She, like so many other executives, was a very busy manager who viewed writing e-mails and having personal conversations as a burden. However, the time it took people to come back to her for clarity was longer than the time it would have taken for her to focus and articulate in the first place.

So yes, communicating with clarity takes time, but it's like the time needed to construct the foundation of your home. If you do it right the first time, you don't waste time going back and making repairs. Would you build your house on a bed of sand? Of course you wouldn't. But that's what you're doing if you neglect the all-important role clear communication plays in making you and your company successful.

Passionate communication

Whatever words we utter should be chosen with care,
for people will hear them and be influenced by them for good or ill.
—Buddha

We're going to talk passion now. Do I have your attention? I thought so! However, I'm not talking about the kind of passion that may have immediately come to mind. I'm talking about passionate communication and how important it is to your business. Let's take a look at a longtime friend of mine to drill down on this subject a bit more.

I have had the pleasure of working with Paul for a long time—long enough to know that while he is soft-spoken and reserved, he is also profoundly passionate about his work. Indeed, from our shared history, I can confirm that Paul's emotion and drive are the very cornerstones of his business success. His employees, though, don't share that history. They only know what they experience *now*, so the feedback I got from 360-degree interviews was that Paul comes across as detached and dispassionate. He's far from that, but we both realized that there was a reason his employees perceived him the way they did, and we both knew that had to change. Finding the right balance between reserve and passion in how he communicated with his followers was a major factor in turning things around for Paul.

Communicating with clarity, while important, isn't effective unless you also communicate with passion. *Passion*, I realize, is a somewhat-uncomfortable concept, but I'm not talking about romantic desire or cheerleading. I'm talking about passion as a strong enthusiasm or energy that produces a similar enthusiasm or energy in others. Think about it. Would you follow a laid-back hero over the top of the hill I've mentioned a couple of times already? Can a hero even be laid-back? I think not. A hero will psych you up to follow him or her over the crest of that next ridge in business. You'll follow because you believe. You won't truly believe unless the person you follow believes too. Passion is required to foster that kind of inspiration, that kind of belief.

Ascending executives can easily presume that colleagues and teammates know how much they care about their work and career path. But passion requires action. Unless your emotion is on display, no one knows it's there. When I discussed self-control, I talked about the negatives associated with displaying too much emotion and also the negatives that come to pass if you are too self-controlled and show little or no emotion. In both cases, I suggested a balance is needed. Well, the same balance is needed with passionate communication. Show too little emotion, and your followers won't believe in you. Show too much, and your followers might think you're out of control, even a little crazy. When you exhibit passion with the right balance, people will feed off of your zest, enthusiasm, and energy. Better still, they will contribute your energy to their own.

Unfortunately, an absence of passion leads to apathy. And that's what Paul faced: an apathetic workforce that felt he didn't care and thus thought, *So why should we?*

Communicating with passion requires a high degree of thoughtfulness and self-awareness. You want to make the most of all your communications—verbal, written, and physical. Here's another fun acronym, a bit more alphabet soup for you: APT, which stands for *action*, *precision*, and *tone*—three things you should take into account when communicating.

Action. A large percentage of communication is physical. Be sure that your actions reflect the energy you want to project. If you are trying to generate excitement, for example, you might want to punctuate your points by using hand gestures. If you're trying to maintain someone's interest, it may be best to walk around the stage rather than stand behind a podium. Facial expressions and animation also reinforce your message. Like all good things, though, too much action can backfire. Remember your audience, remember what you're trying to express, and remember to stay authentic. It's all a matter of balance.

Precision. Lengthy sentences, repetitive points, and polysyllabic words all drain the passion from your written and spoken communications. Choose the words that best fit your meaning—for example, *extraordinary* rather than *very good*. (As an aside, when you choose the right word, there's hardly ever a reason to use the word *very*.) Work to find the right balance between droning e-mails and cryptic ones. Like every other behavior, this requires thought and planning—and often the eagle eyes and ears of someone from your personal advisory board. Consider sharing your written action plan with your close allies. If they say your message isn't clear and if there is consistency in the criticism, then you can be sure your message could use some additional clarity. Eliminating business jargon and overly complex sentence structure can help you achieve your objectives.

Tone. Monotone speeches don't promote interest or understanding, much less passion. Your communication should reflect your feeling. Likewise, your volume should be adapted to the circumstances. Bear in mind that if you are too quiet, you can be seen as detached, and if you're too loud (including written communications that are entirely UPPERCASE or in **bold**), you can be seen as overbearing. Unless you're in church or at a football game, you're aiming neither for whispering nor shouting; you simply want to be clear and engaging. Again, it's all a question of balance. Indeed, isn't that true of life in general? The ancient Greek poet Hesiod once wrote, "Observe due measure; moderation is best in all things." In many ways, business reflects most aspects of life. That's something to keep in mind as you continue to assess your leadership behavior with a view toward changing it for the betterment of yourself and all the people who work for you.

Surely to the glee of the Saturday Night Live players, former president Bill Clinton is a master at communicating with passion. Although easily imitated, his style is nonetheless effective. He flings his arms wide, speaks with his palms up, and uses his pointer finger to make a point. He paces his speeches to allow listeners to digest his concepts and appreciate his points. He repeats for effect, not because he's straying off topic. And he modulates his tone and facial expressions to reflect his message. He's the poster child of APT.

Remember my client Paul? As I mentioned, he *was* a passionate leader; he simply needed his energy to come across. So, among the many business issues we discussed, I gave him very specific communication goals. For example, in a one-hour meeting, he was to raise his voice a minimum of three times. He was to raise his hand and tap the table at least twice. Sounds simple, doesn't it? But it also required acting deliberately. And it worked.

As Paul became more animated, his staff began to see him as more energetic, involved, and interested. As Paul communicated his corporate vision with passion—more and more people bought into his vision. I've said this before, and I'll definitely say it again: you have to act the part of a leader. If you don't know your role, you can't be effective onstage.

Communicating your vision

> The two words "information" and "communication" are often used interchangeably, but they signify quite different things. Information is giving out; communication is getting through.
> —Sydney J. Harris

Consider a world without vision. How would you feel? Fearful? Confused? Reticent? Confined?

Of course you would—and the same is true for people in an organization (i.e., followers) whose leaders do not communicate a clear vision. Without a clearly expressed and clearly understood vision, it is only natural that team members fall short of expectations. They are operating, if you will, in the dark.

A great vision is inspiring. It gets everyone excited to come to work. But only—and this is a big *only*—if the vision is clearly communicated to everyone on the team.

Communicating with vision means providing a clear picture of where you want to go; communicating with strategy means describing how to get there. Without vision, you have chaos; without strategy, confusion. Without clarity, you also have confusion, so clarity must precede strategy. Without passion, nobody will care about your vision regarding the way forward to increased productivity and profitability for the company.

In my experience, few people at the top have a clear vision and strategy, and fewer still communicate it. Strong leaders clearly articulate their vision for their team, for their company, and then consistently repeat and communicate that vision until everyone gets it. The most successful leaders not only create a shared vision but also model how to use that vision, looking beyond what appear to be pressing problems, to keep their eyes—and the eyes of their team—on the prize.

A leader communicating with *vision* has perspective, leading to harmony and teamwork. A leader with *strategy* provides a road map to get the entire team going in the same direction.

Let's look back at Elsa from the beginning of this chapter. She had a clear vision in her head of where to take the organization. She knew she had to articulate her vision to the masses. Sometimes leaders will paint a picture (vision) and neglect to describe the strategy to attain the vision. Not only did Elsa have the bigger picture fully conceived, but she also understood the different steps to take to achieve the vision. She understood the components of her business and was able to break down the vision into manageable pieces—the strategy. Elsa was self-aware. She exhibited self-control. She was empathetic, humble, assertive, and effective because she was perceived (correctly) as a person with integrity. Sure, she faced lots of challenges, but she brought the right business behaviors to the party, which is why she triumphed in the end.

As a leader, you have the responsibility to lift the fog, reduce blurriness, and paint a compelling picture of your organization going forward. You have to make sure that everyone can see your vision, and then they have to understand your strategy for achieving that vision.

Communicate your vision with clarity and passion. Talk about it. Write about it. Share it. Share it with the entire organization and then reinforce it—frequently.

Repetition

> The void created by the failure to communicate
> is soon filled with poison, drivel and misrepresentation.
> —C. Northcote Parkinson

Remember Chris, from earlier in this chapter? His boss's curt e-mail left everyone wondering whether his or her job was in jeopardy. But the message itself wasn't the only problem. The other part of the problem was the delay between sending the message and then the explanatory meeting.

Communication without frequency leads to paranoia. When a leader (or a company, for that matter) doesn't have enough communication with his or her team, that team will fill the void with their imaginations. And guess what. Their imaginations never lead them to believe that rainbows and unicorns and pots of gold are just around the corner. Instead, when imaginations run wild, whispering starts, and negative rumors blaze like wildfire.

Consider this progression of thought that I hear on a regular basis from employees of workplaces with infrequent communications: *I haven't heard back from my boss. I don't know if I'm doing what he wants. I don't know what he is thinking. Maybe he found someone else to do it the way he wants. I'm not getting feedback from my board. Oh my God, I'm going to be fired!*

Laugh if you will, but I think each of us can relate. And if you've found yourself in this set of circumstances, I'm willing to bet that nearly every time, you *weren't* fired, there *wasn't* a crisis, and most likely your manager had no idea that you were even slightly rattled.

The issue here is lack of frequency, which may be the most common leadership communication error but, fortunately, may also be the issue most easily addressed. I have a hard time, though, convincing executives to amp up the frequency of their communications, because (1) they have no idea how much employees crave and need communication, (2) they've never considered the many benefits of increased communication, and (3) they themselves don't seem to need it. That's where empathy—addressed earlier in this book—comes in. As a leader, you need to consider what others need and want, not what you would need or want.

Regular communications are not merely for the sake of employees. As I point out to harried executives who claim they don't *have time* to bump up their communication cadence, it's not simply a matter of improving workplace productivity and efficiency. It's about the productivity and efficiency of the message itself. If you really are too busy to communicate, then it's time to appoint someone else to establish a process for communicating on your behalf—frequently, consistently, and properly.

When you communicate with sufficient frequency, you are in control of your message. You are in control of the intended perception and have more effect over the interpretation.

With frequent—and *predictable*—communications, employee confidence and security build. Gossiping and rumormongering fail to thrive in the face of regular corporate communications—even when the news isn't positive. In fact, if the news you're sharing isn't good—say it's about a plant closing or downsizing—employees who feel well informed might jump in to help or at least help control the downward spiral of negative talk throughout the organization.

There's no magic number regarding frequency. What's important is that you consider the intellectual hunger of your recipients, the size of the organization, and the form of communication, because, to say it once again, the best leaders rely on a combination of written, spoken, and physical communication. You'll know you're falling short if people can't repeat what you told them or they repeat the wrong information.

And please, once you establish a level of frequency—whatever that may be—*don't back off*, which can be every bit as alarming as insufficient communication.

I once worked with a midsize client ($20 million in revenue) whose president, Wilson, in a surge of goodwill, began a barrage of communication. Every week, he would send a note to the entire organization updating them on their profit margins and goal attainment. Wilson's organization came to rely upon his updates, which was exactly what he had hoped. However, inside of a year, Wilson tired of the regular communications. Busy and preoccupied with the business of the business, Wilson gave up on his frequent communications, believing that they weren't all that important or needed. It didn't take long for Wilson to realize the error of his ways. The entire workforce quickly questioned the lack of e-mails. Although the company was doing very well, in the absence of communication, Wilson's workforce began worrying that he was leaving the company, that the organization was to be sold, and that they all would be laid off.

My advice to Wilson? Pretty simple, really. Resume consistent written communication immediately but perhaps scale back on his overly optimistic goal of updates on a weekly basis. I also suggested he adopt an internal connections process that allowed his executive team to contribute to his communications, helping lighten the load.

Every now and again, I'll meet with a client who protests the idea of frequency, saying, "They'll get tired of hearing from me. I'll lose my effectiveness if I communicate too much." To me, this is a sham argument. Frequent communication is not nagging. It's *necessary*. And research backs me up.

As detailed in their article "How Managers Use Multiple Media: Discrepant Events, Power, and Timing in Redundant Communication," Tsedal B. Neeley and Northwestern University's Paul M. Leonardi and Elizabeth M. Gerber found that managers who are deliberately redundant as communicators are able to move their projects forward more quickly and smoothly than those who are not.

Advertisers already know this. Research proves, time and time again, that messages are more effective when repeated. Just think of the advertising slogans you can recall from the decades past. Just Do It. Got Milk? It's Squeezably Soft. We Try Harder. Have It Your Way. You remember these catchy phrases not simply because they were well written but also because you heard them over and over and over again.

The same is true for effective leaders. So reach out. Again. And then again. Extinguish gossip wildfires before they can begin. And open the lines of communication.

There's another reason to focus strongly on communication and on repeatedly conveying your vision for how to move the company forward to accomplish the shared objectives that every member of the team should have: you don't want to breed a silo mentality in the ranks, which can happen pretty fast if you're not looking out for the signs of the silos.

Shared objectives

In agriculture, silos are tall, discrete, stand-alone structures for storing bulk materials. Each silo is its own entity, containing its own grain, functioning independently of the others. Many—if not most—large companies also operate in silos, with each department standing separately from the others, with its own goals, its own budgets, its own agendas.

On the surface, the idea makes sense, but in practice, operating in silos— operating without shared objectives—is damaging and detrimental to successful leadership. If you don't communicate your vision clearly and then repeat the message, your business might fall into the silo syndrome.

In my line of work, I hear about silos all the time. When I administer cultural surveys and employee-opinion interviews, I find the implementation of silo mentality is a constant complaint. "We are in silos. We work in silos. Our department has goals. It doesn't matter how the company does; it matters whether we meet our goals."

When I probe, I hear, "I constantly fight for resources so that I can meet our department goals and objectives." "It's not my fault, it's the other department," and "I'm not paid to make other people look good."

Put that way, the problem is obvious, isn't it? Companies and leaders that do not share objectives—with clarity, passion, and frequency—are doomed to be ineffective and inefficient. They will find it impossible to meet their goals or achieve their vision and strategy.

As mentioned in previous chapters, people behave according to the incentives they are given—whether consciously or unknowingly. When I realize that an organization is falling short in sharing its objectives, I immediately examine its *stated goals*. All too often, I find that the organization's president or CEO, although well intended, has created an unhealthy environment of internal competition by establishing competing goals for executives and their departments.

Many companies begin with mission and vision and try to cascade the goals down to departments and then down to individuals. The problem is mission and vision can't cascade down independent silos in the same way when different entities are rewarded differently. Different rewards—whether compensation, benefits, recognition, or even proximity to executives—set up a situation in which teams that should be working together and collaborating instead find themselves competing against one another.

I'll say it again, because I feel so strongly about this: *failing to create and communicate shared objectives will always lead to inefficiency and suboptimization.* When each unit attempts to reach a solution that is optimal for that unit but not optimum for the organization, the organization suffers, and suboptimization occurs.

Reexamine your rewards-system structure. Ensure that it supports and motivates each individual's and each department's success. Start at the very top, including a rewards structure consisting of compensation, perks, intrinsic rewards (e.g., accolades and exposure), and public recognition. The smoothest-running organizations clearly define the goals of every department and ensure that they do not compete with one another, making for a better work environment, teamwork, shared triumph, and exuberance when the organization succeeds.

Leadership roundup

Most every executive will say that effective communication, both internal and external, is vital to the longevity and efficiency of any company. It's interesting, then, that with such a near consensus as to the importance of communication how many leaders fall short in achieving the optimum balance. Perhaps it's because we all communicate. If we're in business, we can all express ourselves in writing and with the spoken word in most cases. Thus, communication takes a backseat. It's taken for granted. That's the mistake many of us make. We can't take effective communication for granted. We have to constantly work to get our message out with clarity, passion, and precision at frequent intervals.

- After you examine your own way of communication, whether it's in writing or in speech, work to identify ways you can clarify. Seek feedback from teammates, even your direct reports. You might be surprised at how often you think you're right on point but have in fact missed first base. Clarity is king in effective communications.
- Walk the tightrope of passion. Be aware that some emotion must come across both in writing and in speech. Without passion, the message won't get the target audience's attention. Seek to achieve the ideal balance between too little and too much emotion and passion in your written and verbal communication.

- The essence of internal corporate communication is vision and strategy. You must share your vision with clarity, and you must convey with passion your strategy for accomplishing the stated objectives.
- As is the case in sales, repeating the message is vital.
- Making a commitment to clear communications is an essential behavior. Once you begin, the behavior will become second nature.

Chapter 9

Global Intelligence

The brain is like a muscle.
When it is in use we feel very good.
Understanding is joyous.
—Carl Sagan

I had the opportunity to meet with a world-renowned physician, Marcus, following an international forum he'd organized for other physicians. Although our meeting was in a typical suburban coffee shop here in the United States, Marcus's description of the forum transported me to the corners of the world. As we sipped lattes, he elaborated on the demographics and technical aspects of his medical seminars, conjuring up graphic visuals of his international audience and their backgrounds. He praised their perspectives and gave very specific examples of what he learned about—and from—them. I asked Marcus about global intelligence and how it may have been valuable to both his leadership of the conference and his responsibilities in a large health care organization.

He thought carefully before responding. "See my car out there?" Marcus asked, pointing to the parking lot. "It's like me being in that car, and that car is my world of work, which is all good. But if I really want to know about cars, if I want to understand where they fit in the parking lot and how mine is different from or the same as others, then I have to get outside of the car. *I have to see the whole parking lot.* I have to see which cars fit well into certain spaces and which ones don't. I have to look at other cars to see where my car is falling short, or at least where the potential might be in the future. It's a big parking lot. And I have to always be cognizant that there are many, many other cars outside of my space. Does that make sense?"

Of course it made sense. Marcus had to get outside the car. He needed to regard his surroundings. He needed perspective. He needed to understand realms outside of his influence.

Global intelligence defined

> The difference between stupidity and genius is that
> genius has its limits.
> —Albert Einstein

Global intelligence—the awareness of events and situations outside our day-to-day activities and local influence—gives us perspective. By stretching beyond the familiar, ripping open the envelope of our normal, we see and learn new things that can forever impact our own behavior. In short, global intelligence is a heightened sense of world awareness. It's very much akin to self-awareness, except instead of looking inward to seek understanding of yourself, you have to look outward to seek understanding of people and cultures in distant lands. Armed with this knowledge, you can proceed forward with your vision for your company with the assurance that you're not doing so with blinders on. You're part of the global business community, which is a very exciting place to be!

Thomas Friedman, in his book *The World Is Flat*, maintains that societies and businesses are completely interconnected. He further acknowledges that there are barriers—physical, trade, political, ideological—that can be eradicated when we communicate and do business with one another, no matter where we are.

That notion of opening doors and knocking down barriers is, to my way of thinking, global intelligence. Global awareness perpetuates certain excellent leadership behaviors. That is because global awareness feeds empathy (the ability to understand people's thoughts and predict their behaviors). The presumption is that the more aware you are of your local and global world, the more you will understand people around you and the better you will be at influencing and collaborating with them.

Of all the leaders I have coached, some of the most effective at influencing organizations and individuals alike are the ones who have a global mentality. My use of the word *mentality* is deliberate, meaning a way of thinking or the ability to think and learn. As I see it, to have global intelligence, a leader does not need to literally travel around the world. To me, global intelligence is a mind-set—a mentality.

Anyone—or at least anyone who makes a genuine effort—can achieve it.

In my early twenties, I traveled the world extensively and had lived in many places. When I first met my future husband, he had not. I'd traveled to and lived in different countries, experienced different cultures, attended many schools, and was necessarily, keenly aware of world events. My experiences, however, were dwarfed by Bill's self-acquired (not necessarily "experienced") knowledge. Despite my worldly background, I couldn't hold a candle to Bill's awareness of global events, his openness to people's differences, and his understanding of international politics and economies. (I am glad to say that I have caught up, and we continue to make a good team.)

How do the best leaders come to have global intelligence, and at what point does it begin influencing their behavior? Does their acquisition of worldly knowledge lead them to become successful? Or does their drive for global intelligence arise after they became leaders?

Yes. I believe the answer to both of these last two questions is yes.

You have probably heard the old saying "Knowledge is power." Although the saying itself may be trite, like so many sayings, this one is spot on. Knowledge can lead to understanding, which can lead to communication (covered in the previous chapter), which can lead to power. In this case, power means an influential position, another way of describing leadership.

Knowledge is power.

Put another way, *global intelligence is leadership.*

To be clear, global intelligence is *not* about being the smartest kid in the class. Global intelligence has more to do with making an effort to be informed about events and realities outside your usual realm of influence and living, including understanding (similar to empathy) and learning about people who think, live, believe, and operate differently than you.

Global intelligence is about staying connected with the rest of the world. And yes, I get it. You are busy. Demands on your time are great. You have to be efficient. There are only so many hours in a day. Your tendency to focus on the work at hand is only natural.

But here's the problem. Staying focused on your own industry—your own backyard, if you will—can make you narrow-minded, provincial. When problems arise—and they inevitably will—the metaphorical problem-solving well from which you draw is not as deep as it could be. You need greater resources. You need to be sufficiently nimble and agile to adapt to people of different backgrounds, educations, and cultures—people who work in different industries and with different goals and priorities, whether they are customers, shareholders, boards of directors, or teammates.

You need global intelligence.

So don't think about having global intelligence as being the smartest or coolest kid in the class. It's more about being the kid who understands how to connect with all the people in his or her world—with teachers and peers and parents and custodians. The one who glides through school making people feel comfortable and welcome, all while progressing and achieving his or her goals. The one who leads. The one who returns to the high school reunion an unquestionable success.

Benefits of global intelligence

> Intelligence is the ability to adapt to change.
> —Stephen Hawking

During a recent 360-degree feedback process, I interviewed a director of a midsize manufacturing company, Michelle, who, at the time, was two levels below the CEO, which, in her company, is like being in Dante's Limbo—somewhere betwixt and between eternity. I'd seen many similar cases. Michelle might never work her way to the CEO's radar, or she might—just *might*—find a way to break through.

As it turns out, Michelle doesn't have to work at attracting favorable attention. People are drawn to her. In client meetings and on phone calls and even at company retreats, her ability to participate in and contribute to conversations about even the most arcane or breaking-news topics is both uncanny and genuine. She further has a natural interest in international events and issues, even those in less commonly known countries. Michelle isn't showing off, but her far-flung knowledge base puts her in a position to connect with teammates, clients, and superiors. As such, she's become a highly regarded go-to person—an unfailing source of information. It didn't take long before the CEO noticed Michelle's contributions and not much longer before Michelle was promoted into an executive leadership role.

Being globally intelligent greases the track, so to speak. It makes it easier for a leader to show empathy (chapter 4), to show humility (chapter 5), and to communicate (chapter 8). Which is nothing to say about how it obviously makes it easier to conduct international business. Even without the positive influence global intelligence has on other behaviors, just think of all the ways global intelligence can positively affect your business transactions.

From a purely fiscal standpoint, there are benefits to having global intelligence. To secure the confidence of investors, your constituents need to feel that your knowledge extends beyond the boundaries of your business or industry. They know that the global economy can be influenced by the nuances of politics and cultural differences and current events—all of which should be within your grasp.

When I was a very young professional, I landed an enviable position at a large regional company. By this time, I'd been in the United States for ten years—still somewhat tentative and not 100 percent assimilated, but that may have been the least of my concerns. This was life altering—my first real job after undergraduate school. In any company meeting, I was usually the youngest person in attendance. It could have been very uncomfortable, but my natural tendency to observe kicked in, and as I sat in one meeting after the other, reading one memo after the other, I eventually recognized that one executive, Matthew, was particularly strategic and effective.

As I have noted earlier, when I conduct 360-degree interviews, I routinely ask, "Is this leader someone you would follow over a hill, not knowing what's on the other side?" If someone had asked me at that time, there was no question: I would have followed Matthew over any hill. He was intellectual; he was informed; he was aware. I recognized then that Matthew had what I now refer to as global intelligence, and some twenty-five years later, he still does. In fact, looking back, I see that he exhibited many of the positive behaviors mentioned in this book. But clearly, his global intelligence was most prominent.

Globally intelligent leaders keep up with the thinking, progress, and issues of different constituencies—whether they are in agreement or not. Remember the chapter on empathy? Globally intelligent leaders score high in empathy, understanding and predicting other people's thinking, mentality, motivations, and behavior, despite what might appear to be insurmountable differences, such as those that fall into these categories:

Generational. Regardless of their own age, globally intelligent leaders understand and build strong relationships with all generations from millennials to baby boomers.

Thinking. Instead of being threatened by constituents who think differently, globally intelligent leaders appreciate diversity in thinking, recognizing opportunities to expand their knowledge base by surrounding themselves with people who don't necessarily share the same views, personality, or behaviors.

Racial and ethnic. The best leaders know how to appreciate and get along with individuals and groups of different racial and ethnic backgrounds.

Religious. Many successful leaders have strong convictions, some of them quite religious. Even so, I find that globally intelligent leaders are well educated about other people's religions, showing deference for other people's views, choices, and deities, even if they don't hold or haven't been previously exposed to the same beliefs.

These are, of course, but a few of the differences we, as individuals, have to overcome in order to be globally intelligent. And as many differences as there are between individuals, there can be just as many to overcome between teams, departments, and offices—even within the same company.

You surely recognize examples within your own organization, like the engineering teams, the creative teams, the salespeople, and the IT group. Each has its own reputation and style of operating—falling within and outside stereotypes. But a globally intelligent leader can understand the thinking and operating style of each. And *understanding* leads to behaving a certain way. And *behaving* in a certain way leads to successful and effective leadership.

There is, I think, a natural tendency for leaders to surround themselves with people who are similar to themselves, whether in personality, behavior, interests, age, or so on. But if you succumb to that pitfall, you are limiting yourself. You may do fine when times are good, but in times of stress, when business is bad or when you need to achieve greater goals, the well upon which you can draw will be shallow.

If, however, you make a habit of being globally intelligent, then you'll open doors, drawing in people (i.e., followers) with assorted strengths to set the stage for future success and achievements.

Becoming globally intelligent

> I know that I am intelligent because
> I know that I know nothing.
> —Socrates

Early in my career as an executive coach, when I spoke about global intelligence, I was often met with resistance. "I don't have time." "It's not a priority." "There's nothing I can do."

Nowadays, though, there is no excuse. With today's technology, you can Google a client while you're on the elevator up to meet him or her. You can connect with people virtually.

On her way to a pivotal client meeting, one of my clients, Anita, received an e-mail from one of the organization's offices in Beijing giving her a heads-up that the meeting would include an additional Chinese executive. My client was well versed in the cultural differences and nuances between Asian corporate cultures and American corporate cultures. She wasn't, however, up to speed on this particular client's background and reputation. As she traveled by cab to the meeting, she took time to conduct research on her smartphone and later reported to me, "I am so glad I did! Not only was he a highly ranked executive in the company, but he had conducted extensive research and was renowned in his field. Thanks to modern technology, I was able to show due deference and conduct a much more efficient meeting."

Global intelligence includes local awareness. In my experience, leaders fall short in understanding *local* events. I even know—and you may, as well—individuals who sadly pride themselves on not keeping up with their hometown news. How can any leader hope to engage in worldly conversations if he or she isn't aware of what's happening in his or her own backyard?

Nor does gaining global perspective have to be expensive. Yes, there was a time when immersing yourself in a foreign culture or acquiring expertise in an obscure area might be prohibitively expensive, but that is no longer true. Information is available at the click of a button. But only if you decide to seek it out and only when you make it a priority.

Your options, really, are without bounds. You can listen to podcasts, the evening news, and the radio. You can read newspapers and use apps for aggregating the articles most likely to be of interest to you. You can unleash your natural curiosity, asking more questions of people you know well and those you don't.

So stay informed. It's that important. It is part of your job. And in the end, that connection to other people via your global intelligence not only will increase productivity, business, and market share but also your followers' perceptions of you.

Leadership roundup

A sense of the world around you is integral to running your business in the global community. Very few companies operate outside the reach of global influences, even if those influences are indirect. Global awareness feeds your perspective, enabling you to see opportunities that might not exist if you were wearing blinders. It also boosts your ability to empathize with and therefore understand other people. A perpetual curiosity about the world nourishes your mind and spirit, so you can consider the active pursuit of global intelligence part of your personal stewardship. As you can see, all the components of behavior-based leadership fit nicely together into a cohesive package.

- Global intelligence is essentially the act of pursuing the knowledge you need to understand peoples and cultures around the world. You should pursue this knowledge because it will reap immediate benefits for your own business, even if global intelligence doesn't directly impact the bottom line. The benefits include increased empathy for employees, vendors, and clients; nourishment of your mind and spirit through the process of learning; and an opportunity to spot opportunities in international business that might have otherwise eluded you.
- You become globally intelligent when you read books and newspapers and you pay attention to international economic and political news. As you learn, keep an open mind. Remember, not everyone will see the world (and business) the way you do, which is a good thing. Diverse opinions make good companies stronger.
- You have time to become more globally intelligent. Consider it part of your business responsibilities.

Chapter 10

Acting the Part

Don't follow the crowd; let the crowd follow you.
—Margaret Thatcher

Concepts and theories are wonderful when it comes to ascertaining how you can improve your behavior as a leader. Ultimately, though, you have to take action. I often tell my clients that acting like the leader they want to be constitutes the most important action they can take to enhance their effectiveness. Basically, if you can *envision* yourself as a better leader, you'll be well on your way to *being* a better leader. If you act on your vision, you're even better off.

Think of it as if you are an actor on the stage. You learn your lines, you practice your role, and you work with your fellow cast members toward the common goal of creating a performance that the paying audience (your customers) will find satisfying, rewarding, and entertaining. It's not really much of a stretch to extend the metaphor to the world of business. Commerce is the stage. Your company is the cast. You are the director and the producer. If you keep that in mind, you can readily see how acting the part of an effective leader can become a self-fulfilling prophecy. It's like a variation on the famous line from the movie *Field of Dreams*: "If you build it, he will come." Rather, it's more like "If *we* build it together, the *customers* will come."

Success will come! You'll receive rave reviews from your superiors, your colleagues, and your employees. Your people will follow you over that proverbial hill I keep mentioning. They'll do so because they believe in you and your vision. They'll believe you because you put on a convincing performance based on the main components of behavior-based leadership—self-awareness, self-control, empathy, humility, integrity, personal stewardship, communication, and global intelligence. Don't be bashful about seeing yourself as an actor. Revel in your role!

Leaders as actors

> Leadership has been defined as the ability to
> hide your panic from others.
> —Anonymous

It's now time to step onto that stage, out into the spotlight, and *perform*. Stop talking, stop thinking, stop planning, stop consulting, and start *acting*. Did the word *acting* catch you off guard? Does it seem disingenuous to *act* a certain way, as opposed to *being* a certain way?

I understand. We all want to think and believe that our behavior is authentic—that we are true to ourselves. We don't want to think that we are acting. We want these behaviors to seem—and be—natural. However, whether we know it or not, each of us is already performing. How you behave at work is surely different from how you behave at home or on a playing field or on an airplane. You might feel 100 percent free expressing your emotions at home, but in an office elevator, that's likely not the case. You might use gestures and words at your adult softball games that you'd never use at your five-year-old daughter's soccer team.

Work is not your only world. It is only one of many worlds in which you operate. In fact, within any one of those worlds, you may function in many different ways. At home, I am a wife, mother, daughter, dog owner, housekeeper, bill payer, and occasional cook. At your office, you may be a CEO, a colleague, a mentor, a hiring manager, and a friend. My point is that we all operate in a number of worlds, and the way we function on each of those stages is, well, performing.

As a performer at work, part of your role is determined by your title—CEO, project manager, engineer, neurosurgeon. Part of your role is determined by your responsibilities—planning, coding, hiring, designing. Part of your role is based on others' perceptions of you. You already adapt to fit the part. And since that's the case, you are already— whether you know it or not—*performing.*

Please don't get hung up on semantics. *Performing*, in the truest sense of the word, means *fulfilling your duties.* And there is no denying that it is your duty to be a successful, productive, inspiring leader. If you simply can't see yourself as a performer, consider yourself a marketer, packaging and presenting your messages so they have the desired outcome.

You can do this. You have the tools—they are outlined in every chapter of this book. More importantly, you have the desire. Otherwise, why would you have read up to these final pages?

Still, when I am coaching, the notion of performing elicits resistance. People bristle at being told, "Fake it till you make it." And with that particular word choice, I would be uncomfortable as well. Still, in all my years of coaching, I've found that the best leaders know how to behave their way to the top. I know that acting yourself into being a leader is far more easily accomplished than thinking yourself into being a leader.

Over lunch one fall afternoon, a friend of mine, Henry, crystallized for me the necessity and reality of performing. His perspective is pretty unique, as he is both a software developer and trained actor. As I said, pretty unique! Since Henry is so self-aware, he is entirely cognizant of the role acting plays in his day-to-day workplace interactions. In his words, "Walking into work is walking onto stage for me. I deliberately and thoughtfully consider my 'script,' adapt my behavior based on who

I'm talking to, and am fully aware that my appearance and demeanor speak on my behalf."

For decades, the Disney Corporation has trained its leadership diligently, instilling the notion that when its employees are at work—whether in theme parks or in a boardroom—they are on stage. Few visitors to Disney World or Disneyland can dispute the magical and excellent customer service.

What does this mean to the rest of us? Does it mean we turn into actors every time we get into the workplace? Does it mean we are not authentic or true to ourselves? No. It simply means that we are expected to adapt to our environment in a positive way to encourage excellent interpersonal relationships, no matter how we feel. Good actors will tell you that their training includes putting themselves into others' shoes in order to be able to portray a character. In other words, an actor performs with empathy. In fact, for the sake of clarity, we can even take the comparison a step further. Consider, for example, the things an actor must consider every time he or she is on stage.

Set. For an actor, this is where the action happens. In your working environment, your set might include your office, your industry, and your company's vision, mission, and values.

Plot. As a leader, your storyline is a combination of what happens to you and, more importantly, what you do to affect change. Especially in a fast-moving digital, technological, and global era, we are faced with constant change. Your plot thickens, expands, and takes many twists as you adapt to changing market demands, technology, mergers and acquisitions, disaster shares, and so on, not to mention interpersonal relationships.

Role. An actor plays a character. As a colleague, teammate, leader, and/ or subordinate, you also have a persona. You can accept how you are perceived, or, like an actor, you can shape how you portray yourself, to influence, motivate, and inspire those around you. To take the analogy a step further, just as a successful actor can perform many roles, you too have many roles. Outside of the office, you may be a parent, a coach, a sibling, a volunteer, a fan. In the workplace, you assume the role of leader and sometimes that of a follower.

Script. While most actors have to stay true to a written script, as a leader, you have the freedom to write your own script. When you divert from your script, you are winging it, a phrase that comes from the theatre. When actors on stage forget their lines, they look for cues from their colleagues in the wings—hence the term. Refer to chapter 8, "Communication," for tips on communicating clearly and effectively.

Costume. I touched on the importance of attire in chapter 2, "Self-Awareness," because like it or not, your wardrobe is a costume. There is a psychology to the colors you wear, the styles you choose. Your grooming, your accessories, and even your shoes send a message, just as they do for an actor on stage.

Rehearsal. Practice. Practice, practice, *practice.* There comes a point when an actor stops reading his or her lines, learning the cues, and preparing for the role. Whether the actor believes he or she is ready or not, it is time to *assume* the role. No amount of thinking or preparation can replace *action.* Put differently, no amount of good intentions or planning can replace *behavior.*

There will be those among you who still say, "Acting is disingenuous." So let me reframe it with a few more examples: When you are delivering bad news to your team or company and you frame the situation without showing how upset you are, that is acting. If you have a disagreement at home in the morning but go into work and behave as if nothing happened at home, that is acting. If you are tired or in pain and you still walk the halls of your organization to interact with your team and contribute to meetings, that is acting. You are performing your job and performing the role you intend to take on.

Think of the most powerful and highly regarded leaders in the world—
US presidents. Regarded as the leader of the free world, an American
president is privy to state secrets and classified information that would
boggle and horrify the minds of many of us. Almost to a tee, US
presidents are among the most gifted actors in the world. Acting is
practically a job requirement and perhaps one reason that Ronald Reagan
(a classically trained Hollywood actor) was able to be so successful in
his role as US president.

Or consider an example from outside the workplace. Let's say you're
traveling with your family to Paris. It would be entirely natural—if not
expected—for you to learn a few key phrases. *Bonjour. Au revoir. Merci
beaucoup. Ou est le bistro? Je voudrais du vin rouge.* Why do you do this?
You are not French. Do you, for one minute, think you are actually
pulling the wool over the eyes of your Parisian waiter? And the waiter,
is he deluded into believing that French is your native tongue? Of course
not. But does that mean that you are being disingenuous? Of course
not. You're making the effort because you are trying to connect. You
are behaving in a certain way—you are *performing*—in order to make
an impression and to be understood.

Jessica, a medical professional, is extremely inquisitive, educated,
enlightened, and, paradoxically, laid-back. In meetings, she speaks so
rarely that some of her colleagues might not even recognize her voice.
Not that she isn't constantly thinking. So far as I can tell, Jessica's
mind is always whirring—in constant motion. She thinks and thinks
and thinks. And internalizes and internalizes and internalizes. Her
colleagues have no idea that anything is weighing heavily on her mind.
She's laid-back Jessica until *boom!* Completely out of context—at least,
for the people around her—Mount Jessica erupts.

As I learned in 360-degree interviews, coworkers feel that Jessica
needs to exhibit more passion, charisma, and predictability in her
communications. I've been coaching her as to what is expected, and
being the very bright person she is, Jessica caught on right away. But she

still struggled to take the next step. Even with specific instructions—"Speak up at least four times during a meeting. Ask a coworker about his or her weekend."—she couldn't convincingly get her colleagues to see her as anything other than laid-back, disengaged Jessica. Eventually, I asked her, "Who do you admire? Name another leader you wish you could be more like."

Without hesitating, Jessica immediately named a few leaders—within and without her company. And just as quickly, she identified one leader in particular whom she regards as a role model. From here, my job was easy. "Imagine that person's behaviors," I told her. "The next time you're in a high-pressure or difficult situation, imagine what that person would do. And then—whether it feels natural or not—*do it. Assume that persona. Act like the leader you want to be.*"

Curtain call

> The greatest leader is not necessarily the one who does
> the greatest things. He is the one that gets the
> people to do the greatest things.
> —Ronald Reagan

Actors inspire. They call up the deep emotions within us all. I understand that the process can be scary. Who really wants all that power anyway? These sentiments come up more often than you might think. Hours and hours into the coaching process, an executive will say, "I've changed my mind. I'm not ready. I don't want to do this." Sometimes the executive will back out while simultaneously insisting that his or her team stay the course. The reason? Most of the time it is, in theater parlance, good old-fashioned stage fright—the fear of suffering negative repercussions, missing your cues, or coming across as foolish or incompetent. An actor, though, would be the first to tell you that no amount of talking or thinking will help you overcome these fears. You just have to step out on that stage and do it. Don't expect perfection the first time out of the gate. Just keep at it. With practice, your behavior will become second nature. And stage fright will become a thing of the past.

When my friend Henry decided in college that he might want to pursue a career other than acting, he wasn't entirely sure where else he might be successful. Technology seemed appealing and suited his tremendous skill set, but getting into the engineering school required a personal interview. He shared his apprehension about the interview process with a fellow actor friend, who promptly responded, "Dude, you can do it. You're an *actor*."

Years ago, I had the opportunity to speak—for three minutes—in front of a highly regarded leader. In preparation for those three minutes, I practiced for hours—in front of friends or in front of the mirror. I didn't keep count, but I likely put three hundred minutes of preparation into those three minutes ... which went very well! To this day, I have no regrets about my performance. I accomplished everything I'd intended.

Behaviorists sometimes call this *social skills training*. An individual with social anxiety or introversion, for example, might be encouraged to (1) observe other socially skilled individuals, (2) practice ("rehearse"), and (3) gather feedback.

Again, some clients protest that this is not authentic, to which I have to respond that being authentic isn't always productive or effective. If you're in a bad mood, if you're off your game, if you're tired of the daily grind, then being your authentic self and wearing those feelings on your sleeve is going to be counterproductive. Performing helps you mask negative feelings.

Do not get caught up in the semantics of *acting* and *being honest* either. If your best friend meets you for lunch with a fresh haircut that is, in your opinion, horrendous, are you going to tell your friend, "I think your hair is horrendous"? Of course not. You're going to choose your words wisely. You are going to act. You are going to market your message. You are going to respond with social skills.

As you begin to take steps I've suggested in previous chapters to change your behavior, note that overcorrection is part of the process. Expect it. When you suddenly behave with more empathy, you may, on occasion, be guilty of being overly empathetic. When you embrace self-control, people may be wary. This is normal. No actor learns his or her craft overnight; it takes practice and training. As you look to find your new self as a leader, your followers may be unsure of what is happening. I urge you to stay the course.

In my experience, nearly all leaders have goodness in them. They have what it takes to succeed. They merely need to peel away the negative behaviors and let the positive behaviors emerge.

So now, get started. You have the tools you need to perform. Presume a posture, a tone of voice, a cadence that reflects your goals and intentions. Change your behavior, and change the results. *Act* like the leader you want to be. *Behave* like the leader you want to be.

Become the leader you want to be.

Bibliography

Chapter 1, "Behavior"

Bennis, W., D. Goleman, and J. O'Toole. *Transparency: How Leaders Create a Culture of Candor.* San Francisco: Jossey-Bass, 2008.
This book encourages leaders to create a culture of honesty, openness, and communication; without clarity and transparency, structure falls apart.

Goldsmith, M. *What Got You Here Won't Get You There.* New York: Hyperion, 2007.
As one of the pioneers in leadership coaching, Goldsmith guides high-achieving leaders to polish their skills and develop self-awareness. His book challenges the reader to analyze where he or she is, where he or she wants to be, and which changes to make to get there.

Hill, N. *Think and Grow Rich.* Seattle: Pacific Publishing Studio, 2009.
In this book, originally published in 1937, Hill details the "Law of Success," which includes steps to achieve goals through belief in one's own success. Hill references success stories of some of the most successful millionaires of his generation, such as Andrew Carnegie, Thomas Edison, and Henry Ford.

Kello, J. E. "Reflections on I-O Psychology and Behaviorism." In *Reflections on Adaptive Behavior: Essays in Honor of J. E. R. Staddon,* edited by N. K. Innis. Cambridge, MA: MIT Press, 2008.

An overview of the impact of behaviorism and behavioral psychology in general on the science and practice of industrial-organizational psychology.

Lombardi, V. *What It Takes to Be Number #1: Vince Lombardi on Leadership.* New York: McGraw-Hill Professional, 2003.
An overview of famed football coach Vince Lombardi's philosophy of leadership, written by his son Vince Lombardi Jr.

Maxwell, J. C. *Leadership 101: What Every Leader Needs to Know.* Nashville, TN: Thomas Nelson, 2001.
One of Maxwell's many little books on leadership, all of which are enlightening.

Chapter 2, "Self-Awareness"

"DISC Overview." DISCProfile. https://www.discprofile.com/what-is-disc/overview/.
This overview provides a general explanation of the DISC instrument, a leading personal assessment tool used to improve work productivity, teamwork, and communication.

Gonzales, M. *Mindful Leadership: The 9 Ways to Self-Awareness, Transforming Yourself, and Inspiring Others.* Mississauga, ON: John Wiley & Sons Canada, 2012.
A resource book that recommends meditative techniques as an aid to increased self-awareness and ultimate effectiveness for leaders.

Peiperl, M. "Getting 360-Degree Feedback Right." *Harvard Business Review*, January 2001.
A general review of the 360-degree interview process.

Zenger, J., and J. Folkman. "Getting 360 Degree Reviews Right." *Harvard Business Review*, September 7, 2012. https://hbr. org/2012/09/getting-360-degree-reviews-right/.
A quick how-to guide to effective 360-degree reviews.

Chapter 3, "Self-Control"

Bialobzeskyte, Agota. "Moral Licensing: How Being Good Can Make You Bad." *Pick the Brain* (blog). August 18, 2013. http://www.pickthebrain. com/blog/moral-licensing-how-being-good-can-make-you-bad/.
Bialobzeskyte provides examples of how moral licensing can ruin our efforts to change despite our best intentions.

Blanken, I., N. van de Ven, and M. Zeelenburg. "A Meta-Analytic Review of Moral Licensing." *Personality and Social Psychology Bulletin* 41, no. 4 (2015): 540–58.
An up-to-date summary of findings from numerous research studies about moral licensing, supporting the idea of a potential downside of doing something positive, namely the problem of giving oneself permission to now do something negative.

Collins, J. C. *How the Mighty Fall: And Why Some Companies Never Give In*. New York: HarperBusiness, 2009.
Collins explains that decline in companies is often self-inflicted, stemming from the initial denial of risk and peril. However, when leaders address risks and take recovery of their companies into their own hands, companies can come back even stronger.

Collins, J. C., and M. T. Hansen. *Great by Choice: Uncertainty, Chaos, and Luck—Why Some Thrive Despite Them All*. New York: Harper Business, 2011.
Another classic by renowned author Jim Collins. This one emphasizes the importance of self-discipline in leadership of successful companies.

Drucker, P. F. "Managing Oneself." *Harvard Business Review*, January 2005.

The renowned leadership and management author P. F. Drucker gives his thoughts on the importance of self-management.

McGonigal, K. *The Willpower Instinct: How Self-Control Works, Why It Matters, and What You Can Do to Get More of It*. New York: Avery, 2012.

An excellent in-depth review of self-control as a key variable in leader success.

Mischel, W. *The Marshmallow Test: Mastering Self-Control*. New York: Little, Brown, 2014.

A recap of decades of research on the phenomenon of self-control as demonstrated by the famous marshmallow test, first developed by the author.

Chapter 4, "Empathy"

Carnegie, D. *How to Win Friends & Influence People*. New York: Simon & Schuster, 1936.

The classic source for understanding the fundamentals of building relationships.

Covey, S. R. *The 7 Habits of Highly Successful People: Powerful Lessons in Personal Change*. New York: Simon & Schuster, 1989.

A classic book that strongly emphasizes the role of empathy as a critical success factor.

Lyons, R., H. A. Priest, J. L. Wildman, E. Salas, and D. Carnegie. "Managing Virtual Teams: Strategies for Team Leaders." *Ergonomics in Design: The Quarterly of Human Factors Applications* 17 (2009): 8–13.

A review of intentional strategies that help leaders build and lead global virtual teams made up of members of various ethnicities and geographies.

Stephan, W. G., and K. Finlay. "The Role of Empathy in Improving Intergroup Relations." *Journal of Social Issues* 55, no. 4 (1999): 729–43.
Research study indicating the role of empathy in reducing misperception and prejudice and providing strategies for increasing empathy in heterogeneous groups.

Watkins, M. D. *The First 90 Days: Proven Strategies for Getting up to Speed Faster and Smarter.* Cambridge, MA: Harvard Business School Press, 2013.
Strategies for effective onboarding, centering on the role of empathy.

Chapter 5, "Humility"

Collins, J. C. *Good to Great: Why Some Companies Make the Leap … and Others Don't.* New York: Harper Collins, 2001.
A classic study of companies that experienced a dramatic improvement in their business performance, as tied to the qualities of their leaders. Perhaps surprisingly, the "Level 5" leader is a servant-leader, marked by humility.

Dotlich, D. L., and P. C. Cairo. *Why CEOs Fail: The 11 Behaviors That Can Derail Your Climb to the Top and How to Manage Them.* San Francisco: Jossey-Bass, 2003.
A behavior-focused prescriptive look at leader behaviors that misfire, including arrogance and lack of humility.

Pagoto, S. "Are You a People Pleaser? How the Inability to Say 'No' Can Lead to Health Consequences." *Psychology Today.* October

26, 2012. https://www.psychologytoday.com/blog/shrink/201210/
are-you-people-pleaser.
Pagoto addresses the consequences that can arise from people-
pleasing, such as a decrease in health and increase in anxiety. She
addresses the reasons people people-please, which include fear of
rejection and fear of failure.

Winch, G. "Do You Have an Arrogant Boss? The Psychology of
Horrible Bosses." *Psychology Today.* July 30, 2012. https://
www.psychologytoday.com/blog/the-squeaky-wheel/201207/
do-you-have-arrogant-boss.
Stanley Silverman (University of Akron) et al. developed a scale to
measure manager arrogance and identified the primary behaviors
bosses engage in that are damaging to their organizations. The
article also details how to handle a boss who is arrogant.

Chapter 6, "Integrity"

Owen, J. P. *Cowboy Ethics: What Wall Street Can Learn from the Code
of the West.* Ketchum, ID: Stoeklein, 2004.
Ethical principles of the Old West, as applied to contemporary
business (and especially financial institutions).

Plemon, J. "Why Integrity Is Important in the Workplace."
Seed Time (blog). October 22, 2012. http://christianpf.com/
why-integrity-is-important-in-the-workplace/.
This blog entry, based on the book, *The Millionnaire Mind* by
Thomas J. Stanley, describes how honesty and integrity ultimately
contribute to the overall health and success of a business.

Silverstein, K. "Enron, Ethics and Today's Corporate Values." *Forbes.* May
14, 2013. http://www.forbes.com/sites/kensilverstein/2013/05/14/
enron-ethics-and-todays-corporate-values/.

Article highlighting the failures of ethically challenged—even crooked—companies (such as Enron).

Sonnenfeld, J. A., and A. J. Ward. *Firing Back: How Great Leaders Rebound after Career Disasters.* Boston: Harvard Business School Press, 2007.
Based on many years of research, the authors identify strategies that leaders can use to recover and rebuild their reputations after even devastating losses.

Chapter 7, "Personal Stewardship"

Bryant, Yura. "How Your Health Affects Your Business." *Huffington Post*, September 30, 2015. http://www.huffingtonpost.com/yura-bryant/how-your-health-affects-y_b_8220164.html.
Bryant provides three simplistic steps to improve personal health, which could ultimately impact your business's success.

Fischer, M.A., N. K. Choudhry, G. Brill, J. Avorn, S. Schneeweiss, D. Hutchins, J. N. Liberman, T. A. Brennan, and W. H. Shrank. "Trouble Getting Started: Predictors of Primary Medication Nonadherence." *American Journal of Medicine* 124, no. 11 (2011): 1081.e9–22. See also Fischer, M. A., M. R. Stedman, J. Lii, et al. "Primary Medication Non-Adherence: Analysis of 195,930 Electronic Prescriptions." *Journal of General Internal Medicine* 25, no. 4 (2010): 284–90.

Intlekofer, K. A., and C. W. Cotman. "Exercise Counteracts Declining Hippocampal Function in Aging and Alzheimer's disease." *Neurobiology of Disease* 57 (2013): 47–55.
This abstract reports that animal and human studies show exercise provides a powerful stimulus to counteract molecular changes underlying the progressive loss of hippocampal function in advanced age and Alzheimer's Disease.

Kopp, S. B. *If You Meet the Buddha on the Road, Kill Him! The Pilgrimage of Psychotherapy Patients.* Palo Alto, CA: Science and Behavior Books, 1972.

In this classic self-help treatise, Kopp argues that no one can give you the answers to your life or your own success. You need to develop an internal locus of control, taking control of your own path to personal/interpersonal success.

Laozi. *Tao Te Ching: The Way.* 1900.

A manual-style "Book of the Way" that teaches how to be in touch with the self and the Tao (basic principles of the universe) to become a balanced and serene being. There are many English-translation versions.

Reynolds, G. "How Exercise Could Lead to a Better Brain." *New York Times Magazine*, April 18, 2012. http://www.nytimes.com/2012/04/22/magazine/how-exercise-could-lead-to-a-better-brain.html?_r=0.

Scientists have gathered evidence supporting the conclusion that exercise prevents shrinkage of the brain and can enhance cognitive flexibility. Research also indicates that we have the ability to generate new brain cells through neurogenesis (contrary to the popular belief that we are born with a certain number of brain cells).

von Thiele Schwarz, U., and H. Hasson. "Employee Self-Rated Productivity and Objective Organizational Production Levels: Effects of Worksite Health Interventions Involving Reduced Work Hours and Physical Exercise." *Journal of Occupational and Environmental Medicine* 53, no. 8 (2011): 838–44.

An empirical study showing that reducing work hours can to some extent promote employee health and at the same time promote higher productivity.

Chapter 8, "Communication"

de Vries, R. E., A. Bakker-Pieper, and W. Oostenveld. "Leadership = Communication? The Relations of Leaders' Communication Styles with Leadership Styles, Knowledge Sharing and Leadership Outcomes." *Journal of Business & Psychology* 25, no. 3 (2010): 367–80.
A research study that found that the most-effective leadership styles were associated with the highest and most-positive styles of communication by the leader.

Gleeson, B. "The Silo Mentality: How to Break Down the Barriers." *Forbes*. October 2, 2013. http://www.forbes.com/sites/brentgleeson/2013/10/02/the-silo-mentality-how-to-break-down-the-barriers/.
This *Forbes* article describes how interdepartmental turf wars are destructive to an organization and are a result of a conflicted leadership team. It offers suggestions for leaders on how to break down silos and rebuild a common and unified vision where all parts of the organization can work toward achieving a common goal.

Leonardi, P. M., T. Neeley, and E. M. Gerber. "How Managers Use Multiple Media: Discrepant Events, Power, and Timing in Redundant Communication." *Organization Science* 23, no. 1 (2012): 98–117.
A research study that examined the ways in which leaders widely use redundant communication in various media, especially in times of challenge to reach goals.

Miller, K. *Organizational Communication: Approaches and Processes.* 7th ed. Stamford, CT: Cengage Learning, 2015.
A comprehensive text on communication in the organizational setting.

Chapter 9, "Global Intelligence"

Friedman, T. L. *The Lexus and the Olive Tree: Understanding Globalization*. New York: Farrar, Straus & Giroux, 1999.
The author argues that globalization is a driving force of change in the world, affecting all cultures.

Kemp, L. J., and P. Williams. "In Their Own Time and Space: Meeting Behavior in the Gulf Arab Workplace." *International Journal of Cross Cultural Management* 13, no. 2 (2013): 215–35.
A cross-cultural study of varying norms of behavior in the context of business meetings.

Phillips, K. W. "How Diversity Works." *Scientific American,* October 2014.
Documents the extraordinary value of diversity in group work—how being around people who are different from us makes us more creative, more diligent, more hardworking, and ultimately more successful.

Quappe, S., and G. Cantatore. "What Is Cultural Awareness, Anyway? How Do I Build It?" *The Culturosity Group.* Last modified November 2, 2007. http://www.culturosity.com/articles/whatisculturalawareness.htm.
A general overview of cultural awareness, what it is, how to build it, and the benefits of greater cultural awareness.

Chapter 10, "Acting the Part"

Boegels, S. M., and M. Voncken. "Social Skills Training versus Cognitive Therapy for Social Anxiety Disorder Characterized by Fear of Blushing, Trembling, or Sweating." *International Journal of Cognitive Therapy* 1, no. 2 (2008): 138–50.

A research study demonstrating the effectiveness of strategies that focus on acting in order to effect lasting behavioral change.

Covey, S. R. *Principle-Centered Leadership*. New York: Simon & Schuster, 1991.
An inspiring summary of Covey's principles of leadership, which apply to personal life as well as the organizational world.

Goldsmith, M. *Triggers: Creating Behavior That Lasts—Becoming the Person You Want to Be*. New York: Crown Business, 2015.
Full of revealing stories from Goldsmith's work with chief executives in the business world, *Triggers* offers a personal playbook on how to actually make the changes you need to make to be the person you want to be.

Howell, J. P., and D. L. Costley. *Understanding Behaviors for Effective Leadership*. 2nd ed. Upper Saddle River, NJ: Pearson Prentice Hall, 2006.
A brief but comprehensive look at leader behaviors and how they can influence followers and effect change. An academic text.

Maxwell, J. C. *The 21 Irrefutable Laws of Leadership: Follow Them and People Will Follow You*. Nashville: Thomas Nelson, 1998.
Another of Maxwell's classics, overviewing what he sees as enduring principles of leadership and encompassing much of what is detailed in this book.

Acknowledgments

Thank you to my clients. I am indebted to you for the lessons and stimulating conversations over the years, and I am overwhelmed by your steadfast partnership and trust.

Thank you to my mentor, adviser, and colleague John Kello, PhD, whose wisdom, business savvy, and experience helped me build a strong foundation. It is obvious why you are such a successful consultant and professor! Your patience and generosity are boundless.

Thank you to my phenomenal editor, Cheri Wiles of All Write. I couldn't have done this without you. You helped me navigate the nuances of written communication and taught me the gift of written expression. I will miss our coffee meetings but will cherish our friendship. Any author, new or experienced, would be lucky to have your guidance and perspective.

Terry Cox, thank you for your unwavering support and no-nonsense advice. Ana Naranjo Lothspeich of Strategy Consulting, I appreciate your constant reassurance and social media expertise. Laura Kello, thank you for the last-minute and diligent help with the manuscript.

And special thanks to my family and advisory board: Bill, Katrina, Michelle, Paul, Samia, George, Kim, Caroline, and James. In ways you know and in many more that you don't, each of you has shared wisdom, inspiration, support, and love that has sustained and encouraged me in the writing of this book. Thank you.

Open Book Editions
A Berrett-Koehler Partner

Open Book Editions is a joint venture between Berrett-Koehler Publishers and Author Solutions, the market leader in self-publishing. There are many more aspiring authors who share Berrett-Koehler's mission than we can sustainably publish. To serve these authors, Open Book Editions offers a comprehensive self-publishing opportunity.

A Shared Mission

Open Book Editions welcomes authors who share the Berrett-Koehler mission—Creating a World That Works for All. We believe that to truly create a better world, action is needed at all levels—individual, organizational, and societal. At the individual level, our publications help people align their lives with their values and with their aspirations for a better world. At the organizational level, we promote progressive leadership and management practices, socially responsible approaches to business, and humane and effective organizations. At the societal level, we publish content that advances social and economic justice, shared prosperity, sustainability, and new solutions to national and global issues.

Open Book Editions represents a new way to further the BK mission and expand our community. We look forward to helping more authors challenge conventional thinking, introduce new ideas, and foster positive change.

For more information, see the Open Book Editions website:
http://www.iuniverse.com/Packages/OpenBookEditions.aspx

Join the BK Community! See exclusive author videos, join discussion groups, find out about upcoming events, read author blogs, and much more! http://bkcommunity.com/

strength finders

Start with Why

Edwards Brothers Malloy
Oxnard, CA USA
March 31, 2016